I0007941

Social Media Handbook for Law Enforcement:

Strategies for Public Engagement, Crisis Communication, and Digital Trust

2nd Edition
2025

A comprehensive guide to effective social media use in modern policing, covering engagement strategies, misinformation management, cybersecurity, and ethical best practices.

Introduction

Why a 2nd Edition?

Social media is changing the way every business operates—public safety is no different. When this guide was first written in 2014, law enforcement agencies were just starting to understand how social media could help them sidestep traditional media, build trust, and communicate quickly in emergencies. Back then, humor, self-deprecation, and humanizing officers were the primary strategies used to engage the public.

But times have changed. Social media is now a primary news source for most people, misinformation spreads like wildfire, and public perceptions of law enforcement have shifted significantly. The way agencies engage online must evolve, prioritizing professionalism and transparency while still maintaining a strong connection with the communities they serve.

The Evolving Role of Social Media in Law Enforcement

Social media is no longer just a way to share updates—it's a crucial tool for crisis communication, trust-building, and public education. Agencies must now navigate a digital environment where false narratives can take hold in minutes and public expectations for transparency are higher than ever.

Gone are the days when law enforcement could rely solely on traditional press releases. Today, agencies must engage in real-time conversations, correct misinformation, and be a steady voice of authority while avoiding pitfalls that can damage credibility. This doesn't mean officers have to abandon personality altogether, but it does mean balancing engagement with professionalism is more important than ever.

Goals for the 2nd Edition

This updated guide will help agencies:

- **Move beyond humor-based engagement** to build trust through professionalism and credibility.
- **Adapt to new platforms** like TikTok, Instagram Reels, and LinkedIn while using them strategically.
- **Develop crisis communication strategies** that respond quickly and effectively to misinformation.
- **Use social media as an educational tool**, offering crime prevention, public safety information, and community resources.
- **Address cybersecurity threats**, including hacking, deepfakes, and impersonation attempts.

A New Era of Digital Policing

In the early days, law enforcement social media was about getting noticed and gaining followers. Now, it's about maintaining legitimacy and being the first, most reliable source of truth in an increasingly skeptical world. Agencies that fail to evolve will struggle to maintain public trust, while those that embrace best practices will strengthen their community connections and be seen as credible, professional voices in public safety.

This guide will walk you through updated best practices, platform-specific strategies, and real-world case studies to help your agency succeed in today's digital landscape. Whether you're just starting or refining your approach, this book will give you the tools you need to lead the way today and beyond.

Why Agencies Use Social Media

The Shift from PR to Public Trust-Building

There was a time when law enforcement agencies used social media primarily as an extension of their public relations strategy. It was about getting positive stories in front of the community, highlighting good deeds, and occasionally posting a funny meme to humanize officers. That approach worked for a while, but today's digital landscape demands more.

Social media isn't just about engagement—it's about **public trust**. Agencies can no longer afford to be passive participants in online conversations. The public expects law enforcement to be **transparent, responsive, and proactive** in sharing information. When a crisis unfolds, the first place people turn for updates isn't the evening news—it's their phones. If your agency isn't present in that space, someone else will be controlling the narrative.

The Power of Being the First, Best Source of Information

The days of relying solely on traditional media to tell your story are over. Social media allows agencies to communicate directly with the public, bypassing media filters and ensuring the full story gets told. Whether it's a breaking incident, a community update, or an emergency alert, law enforcement must be the **first, most reliable source of information** for their communities.

Key Benefits of Social Media for Law Enforcement:

1. **Speed & Real-Time Updates** – In an emergency, getting accurate information out quickly can save lives. Social media enables instant communication with the public.
2. **Transparency & Accountability** – Agencies that actively share updates, policies, and even mistakes build credibility and trust over time.

3. **Proactive Misinformation Control** – False narratives spread fast. If agencies aren't active on social media, rumors and speculation will fill the void.
4. **Building a Digital Connection with the Community** – Social media isn't just about crime updates; it's about showing the people behind the badge, fostering relationships, and educating the public.
5. **Recruitment & Professional Branding** – Platforms like LinkedIn and Instagram provide opportunities to highlight career paths, attract talent, and demonstrate professionalism.

Meeting the Public Where They Are

Your community isn't waiting for a press release. They're checking Twitter, scrolling through TikTok, and reading Facebook updates. Law enforcement must **meet people where they are**, rather than expecting them to seek out information through traditional channels.

- **Twitter/X:** Fast, concise updates for breaking news and public alerts.
- **Facebook:** Community engagement, longer-form storytelling, and live Q&A sessions.
- **Instagram & TikTok:** Visual storytelling, recruitment, and public safety tips.
- **Nextdoor:** Hyperlocal engagement, crime prevention tips, and neighborhood-specific updates.
- **LinkedIn:** Professional branding, recruitment, and agency leadership visibility.

Social Media: A Necessity, Not an Option

Some agencies still hesitate to embrace social media, fearing backlash or losing control of their message. The reality is, **not having a social media presence doesn't prevent conversation—it just means you're not part of it**. Law enforcement must own its narrative, provide accurate information, and engage in meaningful dialogue with the public.

The agencies that succeed in 2025 will be the ones that treat social media as an **essential tool for public service**, not just a marketing channel. The goal is simple: be present, be professional, and be trusted.

This chapter sets the foundation for how agencies should approach social media in today's digital-first world. In the next chapter, we'll dive into **strategic planning**—how to set goals, define your agency's voice, and develop a roadmap for long-term success.

Building a Strategic Plan

The Importance of a Strategic Approach

A well-planned social media strategy ensures law enforcement agencies remain consistent, adaptable, and effective in their communication. Without a clear plan, agencies risk reactive messaging, inconsistent engagement, and missed opportunities to build public trust.

Key Benefits of a Social Media Strategy:

1. **Consistency in Messaging** – Ensures that all posts align with agency values and policies.
2. **Stronger Community Relationships** – Builds trust through ongoing, meaningful engagement.
3. **Efficient Resource Management** – Allows for better allocation of staff, time, and budget.
4. **Preparedness for Crisis Situations** – Establishes protocols for rapid response to emergencies.
5. **Adaptability to Emerging Trends** – Provides a structured framework while allowing flexibility as platforms evolve.

Establishing Clear Goals and Objectives

A successful strategy starts with clearly defined goals that align with the agency's mission and community engagement priorities.

Setting SMART Goals:

- **Specific** – Define clear objectives (e.g., improve emergency response communication, increase community engagement by 20%).
- **Measurable** – Establish key performance indicators (KPIs) to track progress.
- **Achievable** – Set realistic expectations based on available resources.

- **Relevant** – Ensure goals align with broader agency objectives.
- **Time-Bound** – Establish timelines for evaluation and adjustment.

Assembling an Effective Social Media Team

A strong social media presence requires a dedicated team with defined roles and responsibilities. Having the right personnel in place ensures consistent messaging, timely engagement, and effective crisis response. Agencies should assess their available resources and structure a team that aligns with their strategic objectives.

For a detailed breakdown of ideal social media roles and responsibilities, see *Appendix E: Ideal Social Media Team*

Identifying Your Audience

Understanding your community helps tailor messaging and engagement strategies.

Key Audience Groups:
- **Local Residents** – General updates, safety tips, and community engagement initiatives.
- **Business Owners** – Crime prevention strategies, collaboration opportunities.
- **Media and Journalists** – Press releases, official statements, and fact-checking.
- **Youth and Young Adults** – School partnerships, interactive content, and safety education.
- **Law Enforcement Professionals** – Recruitment efforts, training opportunities, and interagency collaboration.

Choosing the Right Platforms

Different platforms serve different purposes. Agencies should focus efforts where their audience is most active.

Recommended Platforms for Law Enforcement:

- **Facebook** – Community engagement, detailed announcements, event promotions.
- **Twitter/X** – Real-time alerts, emergency notifications, press interactions.
- **Instagram & TikTok** – Visual storytelling, youth engagement, recruitment.
- **Nextdoor** – Neighborhood-specific updates and localized safety tips.
- **YouTube** – Educational videos, live updates, press briefings.

For a detailed breakdown of more emerging platforms and how to utilize them, see *Appendix D: Emerging Platforms*

Developing a Content Calendar

A structured content plan helps maintain consistency and balance different types of posts.

Elements of a Strong Content Calendar:

- **Recurring Themes** – Safety tips, officer spotlights, crime prevention.
- **Emergency Preparedness** – Pre-drafted messages for crisis situations.
- **Community Engagement Posts** – Encouraging two-way interaction with the public.
- **Seasonal Campaigns** – Awareness efforts tied to holidays, events, and local safety trends.

Sample Posting Schedule:

- **Monday:** Public safety tips.
- **Tuesday:** Officer and department highlights.
- **Wednesday:** Crime prevention education.
- **Thursday:** Community event promotions.
- **Friday:** Engagement-driven content (Q&A, polls, challenges).
- **Saturday/Sunday:** Recaps and notable updates.

For more help with planning content see *Appendix B: Social Media Worksheets*

Measuring Success and Refining Strategy

Regular evaluation ensures that the agency's social media efforts remain effective.

Key Performance Indicators (KPIs):

- **Engagement Metrics** – Likes, shares, comments, and direct messages.
- **Reach and Impressions** – Number of people viewing posts.
- **Response Time** – Efficiency in answering public inquiries and emergency updates.
- **Community Sentiment Analysis** – Monitoring public perception and feedback.
- **Crisis Management Effectiveness** – How well social media was used during an emergency.

The Road Ahead

A strategic, adaptable social media plan is essential for effective law enforcement communication. By defining clear goals, selecting appropriate platforms, and staying informed about emerging trends, agencies can foster long-term engagement and public trust.

Creating Engaging Content

Introduction

Social media is a powerful tool for law enforcement agencies to build trust, enhance transparency, and engage with the community. Well-crafted content can humanize officers, educate the public, and increase awareness of safety initiatives. This chapter provides strategies for creating diverse, engaging, and effective content that resonates with the public.

Building an Effective Social Media Presence

Establishing Clear Goals

A strong social media presence requires clear objectives:

- Increase **public trust and engagement**
- Provide **timely and accurate information**
- Showcase the **human side of law enforcement**
- Combat **misinformation and rumors**
- Encourage **community involvement** in crime prevention

To achieve these goals, agencies should:

- **Develop a content calendar** that balances public safety alerts, community engagement, and educational posts.
- **Use a multi-platform approach** to reach different audiences effectively.
- **Monitor engagement metrics** to refine strategies over time.

The Power of Storytelling in Law Enforcement

Elements of Effective Storytelling

Social media is not just about sharing information—it's about telling a story. Effective storytelling can humanize officers, build trust, and make important messages more relatable.

- **People-Focused Content** – Highlight officers, community members, and positive interactions.
- **Clear and Concise Messaging** – Avoid technical jargon; make posts easy to understand.
- **Emotionally Resonant** – Use narratives that create a connection with the audience.
- **Visually Appealing** – Include high-quality images, videos, or graphics.
- **Call to Action** – Encourage engagement, whether it's asking for tips, feedback, or shares.

Types of Content to Post

A diverse content strategy keeps your audience engaged and ensures messaging remains fresh.

1. Community Engagement Posts

- Show officers participating in local events.
- Feature community member recognition or partnerships.
- Highlight initiatives like toy drives, school visits, or safety workshops.

2. Crime Prevention & Public Safety Tips

- Seasonal crime prevention tips (e.g., holiday shopping safety).
- Traffic and pedestrian safety reminders.
- Home security and fraud prevention advice.

3. Officer Spotlights & Behind-the-Scenes

- Introduce officers with short bios and fun facts.
- Show daily routines, K9 teams, or specialized units.
- Highlight training sessions or community outreach efforts.

4. Breaking News & Emergency Alerts

- Timely updates on incidents (without compromising investigations).
- Road closures, weather advisories, and major disruptions.
- Public instructions during active emergencies.

5. Misinformation Corrections

- Address and clarify viral rumors.
- Provide facts in a clear and professional tone.
- Use infographics or short videos to counter false narratives.

6. Recruitment & Career Highlights

- Feature open positions and application deadlines.
- Share success stories of new recruits or long-serving officers.
- Provide insights into academy training and career development.

7. Fun & Lighthearted Posts (When Appropriate)

- Celebrating National First Responder Days.
- Fun community challenges (e.g., dance challenges, fitness initiatives).
- Engaging quizzes or "Throwback Thursday" posts.

For more help with planning content see
Appendix B: Social Media Worksheets

Best Practices for Writing Social Media Posts

Writing Tips:

- **Keep It Short & Direct** – Aim for clarity; avoid long-winded messages.
- **Use a Conversational Tone** – Sound human while maintaining professionalism.
- **Incorporate Hashtags & Mentions** – Use relevant hashtags to expand reach.
- **Encourage Interaction** – Ask questions or prompt discussions.
- **Use Emojis Sparingly** – Adds personality but should remain professional.

Leveraging Visual Content: Images, Videos, and Infographics

Visuals increase engagement and help messages stand out. Here's how to maximize impact:

1. Photos:

- Use high-resolution, well-lit images.
- Capture candid, natural moments over stiff, posed shots.
- Showcase community involvement, not just enforcement.

2. Videos:

- Keep clips under 60 seconds when possible.
- Use captions for accessibility.
- Show step-by-step processes (e.g., "How to Report a Scam").

3. Infographics:

- Use clear, easy-to-read fonts.
- Keep designs simple and informative.

- Highlight key takeaways with bullet points or icons.

Scheduling and Consistency

Posting regularly keeps your audience engaged and your agency top of mind. A content calendar helps maintain consistency.

Suggested Posting Frequency:

- **Daily:** Crime updates, safety tips, engagement posts.
- **2-3x per week:** Officer spotlights, recruitment posts, educational content.
- **As needed:** Emergency alerts, crisis communications.

Growing an Audience & Increasing Engagement

Exclusive Reveals & Social Media Events

Generating anticipation around an agency's social media presence can significantly boost engagement.

- Announcing **new police vehicles, K9 units, or department initiatives** first on social media.
- Hosting **"Behind-the-Scenes" reveal events** where followers get an exclusive first look at new projects.
- Using **teasers and countdowns** to create curiosity before major announcements.

Tweet-Alongs & Virtual Ride-Alongs

A **Twitter/X ride-along** allows agencies to showcase real-time policing without logistical challenges.

- Choose an **officer with good communication skills**.
- Share **photos, short videos, and updates** from various calls.
- Engage with followers by **answering real-time questions**.

Leveraging Local Influencers & Media

- Hosting a **"Celebrity Ride-Along"** with a local influencer to increase visibility.
- Featuring **community leaders in safety PSA videos**.
- Engaging **youth-oriented influencers** to spread awareness on crime prevention and social responsibility.

Sourcing Content from Officers

Law enforcement agencies can enhance their social media presence by leveraging the perspectives and experiences of officers in the field. Encouraging officers to contribute content fosters authenticity, increases transparency, and helps showcase positive community interactions. However, agencies must establish clear guidelines to maintain professionalism and security.

Content Submission Guidelines

- **Identify Key Themes:** Officers should focus on content that highlights community engagement, crime prevention initiatives, and positive interactions with the public.

- **Ensure Professionalism:** All submissions must align with agency policies, avoiding political opinions, personal views, or sensitive case details.

- **Respect Privacy and Legal Considerations:** Officers should not share identifiable information about victims, suspects, or ongoing investigations without prior approval.

- **Prioritize High-Quality Media:** Submissions should include well-lit, high-resolution images or videos with clear audio and captions when necessary.

- **Include Context:** Officers must provide a brief description of the content, including location, event details, and any necessary disclaimers.

Approval and Review Workflow

To maintain consistency and credibility, agencies should establish a streamlined review process before posting officer-submitted content.

Step	Action
1. Officer Submission	Officers submit content to the designated Public Information Officer (PIO) or social media team via an internal submission portal or email.
2. Content Review	The social media team verifies compliance with agency policies, checks for legal concerns, and ensures high-quality presentation.
3. Approval from Supervisors	If required, a supervisor or command staff member reviews the content for additional approval.
4. Scheduling & Posting	Once approved, the content is added to the agency's social media calendar and posted at an optimal engagement time.

5. Performance Monitoring	The social media team tracks engagement metrics and feedback, refining content strategy accordingly.

Encouraging Officer Participation

- **Offer Recognition:** Highlight officers whose content performs well by mentioning them in internal communications or recognizing their contributions in department meetings.

- **Provide Training:** Educate officers on storytelling, photography, and video basics to help them capture engaging content.

- **Use a Dedicated Submission Platform:** Agencies can use cloud-based tools like Google Drive, Microsoft Teams, or agency-specific content portals to streamline content submissions.

- **Create a Content Suggestion List:** Provide officers with ideas on what types of content to capture, such as K9 unit highlights, behind-the-scenes training, community policing efforts, traffic enforcement initiatives, officer wellness activities, outreach programs with local schools, and real-world examples of problem-solving in the field. Agencies can also encourage officers to share day-in-the-life stories, community event participation, or even lighthearted content that showcases positive interactions with residents.

By implementing these strategies, agencies can build a more authentic and engaging social media presence while maintaining professionalism and security.

Conclusion

Creating compelling content is just the beginning. By implementing these strategies, law enforcement agencies can **expand their reach, foster community trust, and enhance public safety messaging**. A successful social media strategy requires:

- A mix of **interactive, multimedia-rich content**.
- Authentic, **community-driven storytelling**.
- A commitment to **real-time communication and transparency**.

By continuously evolving their **social media strategies**, agencies can **stay ahead of digital trends and maintain their role as trusted public safety communicators.**

Public Engagement & Handling Criticism

The Importance of Engagement

Social media isn't just about broadcasting information—it's about fostering a two-way conversation between law enforcement and the public. Engaging with community members builds trust, demonstrates transparency, and allows agencies to address concerns in real time.

Benefits of Engagement:

- **Builds Community Trust** – When agencies interact authentically, the public sees them as approachable and responsive.
- **Corrects Misinformation** – Engaging in conversations helps dispel rumors and ensure accurate information is shared.
- **Encourages Public Participation** – Community members are more likely to contribute tips, share posts, and participate in safety initiatives.
- **Humanizes Law Enforcement** – Responding with professionalism and empathy reinforces the idea that officers are part of the community.

Best Practices for Engaging Online

Respond Promptly & Professionally

- Acknowledge questions and concerns as quickly as possible.
- Use clear, respectful language in all replies.
- If a situation requires an in-depth response, move the conversation to direct messages or provide contact information.

Encourage Constructive Dialogue

- Ask open-ended questions to spark meaningful discussions.
- Highlight positive community contributions and partnerships.
- Promote safety initiatives and invite public feedback on policing efforts.

Use a Consistent and Respectful Tone

- Maintain a balance between professionalism and approachability.
- Avoid sarcasm or humor that could be misinterpreted.
- If a post or comment becomes emotional, focus on facts and solutions rather than engaging in arguments.

Comment Moderation and Managing Online Discussions

Public engagement is a key component of effective law enforcement communication on social media. However, agencies must also establish guidelines for handling comments in a way that fosters constructive dialogue while preventing the spread of misinformation, hate speech, or harmful content.

Establishing a Moderation Policy

A structured approach to comment moderation ensures consistency, transparency, and legal compliance. The following table outlines a tiered response model for handling public interactions on social media.

Social Media Moderation Tiers

Level	Comment Type	Recommended Action
Level 1	Constructive Criticism	Engage professionally, acknowledge concerns, and provide factual responses.
Level 2	Misinformation or False Claims	Correct with verified facts, linking to an official statement or resource.
Level 3	Hate Speech or Threats	Report, document, and remove per platform guidelines. Escalate to investigative teams if necessary.
Level 4	Spam, Advertisements, or Off-Topic Content	Hide or remove under community guidelines.

Protected Government Speech & First Amendment Considerations

Understanding the Limits of Comment Moderation

Government-operated social media pages function as limited public forums, meaning agencies cannot delete comments or block users simply because they express criticism or disagreement. The First Amendment protects the public's right to engage in discussions, including those that may be unfavorable to law enforcement.

Agencies must ensure their moderation policies comply with legal standards while maintaining an environment free from threats, hate speech, or misinformation.

When Can Comments Be Removed?

While government agencies cannot censor criticism, they may remove content under certain conditions:

- **Hate Speech or Threats** – Comments that incite violence, contain threats, or violate platform policies can be removed and, if necessary, reported to law enforcement.
- **Off-Topic or Spam Content** – Agencies can enforce moderation rules that limit off-topic discussions or excessive self-promotion.
- **Misinformation with Public Safety Implications** – False claims that could cause harm (e.g., misinformation about emergency procedures or crime reporting) may be corrected with factual responses, and in some cases, removed.
- **Obscene or Profane Language** – If an agency's posted guidelines prohibit profanity or obscenities, enforcement must be applied consistently.

Establishing Clear Public Comment Guidelines

To maintain transparency and legal compliance, agencies should publicly post their moderation policies. This ensures consistency and protects against claims of viewpoint discrimination. A pinned post on each agency's social media page should include:

- A commitment to open public discourse and respectful engagement.
- Specific rules prohibiting hate speech, threats, and misinformation.
- The agency's right to remove comments violating these guidelines.
- Instructions on how users can appeal moderation decisions.

Handling Challenges to Comment Removal

If a comment is removed or a user is restricted, agencies should document the reason for enforcement. This documentation should include:

- A screenshot of the original comment.
- The specific policy violated.
- Any previous warnings issued to the user.
- A record of any direct communication regarding the enforcement action.

Agencies should be prepared to reinstate comments if a removal decision is challenged and found to be inconsistent with First Amendment standards.

Responding to Controversial Comments

Not every comment requires a response, but agencies should engage strategically when misinformation or public concern arises. Best practices include:

- **Acknowledging Valid Criticism** – When a community member raises a legitimate concern, respond professionally and offer clarification.

- **Correcting False Information** – If misinformation spreads, provide accurate details backed by official sources.
- **Knowing When to Disengage** – If a user is engaging in clear trolling or provocation, avoid escalating the discussion.

By maintaining a fair and legally sound moderation policy, law enforcement agencies can foster an open, transparent dialogue with the public while upholding constitutional protections.

Leveraging Positive Engagement

While managing criticism is crucial, it's equally important to amplify positive interactions that showcase community collaboration and success stories.

Examples of Positive Engagement:

- **Acknowledging Public Support**: Thank community members who share encouraging messages.
- **Highlighting Community Partnerships**: Feature local events, initiatives, and collaborative efforts.
- **Sharing Success Stories**: Post testimonials, officer spotlights, and positive interactions.

Practical Engagement Strategies for Law Enforcement

Host Live Q&A Sessions

- Use Facebook Live, Instagram Live, or Twitter Spaces to engage with the public directly.
- Allow the community to ask questions in real time and provide transparent answers.

Use Polls and Interactive Content

- Conduct polls on community safety concerns.
- Encourage participation through engagement-driven content.

Final Thoughts: The Road Ahead

Engagement is a cornerstone of an effective social media strategy. When done correctly, it strengthens trust, builds connections, and ensures law enforcement agencies remain accessible to the public. By following these strategies, agencies can create an open dialogue with the community and foster long-term relationships based on transparency and trust.

Measuring Success and Strategy

The Importance of Measuring Social Media Impact

An effective social media strategy isn't just about posting content—it's about understanding what works, what doesn't, and continuously improving. Measuring success helps law enforcement agencies refine their approach, maximize engagement, and ensure they're meeting their communication goals.

Key Reasons to Measure Success:

- **Demonstrates Accountability** – Shows stakeholders the impact of social media efforts.
- **Optimizes Content** – Identifies the types of posts that perform best.
- **Enhances Engagement** – Helps agencies understand what resonates with the public.
- **Guides Resource Allocation** – Ensures time and effort are spent on the most effective strategies.

Establishing Success Metrics

Success on social media isn't just about gaining followers—it's about meaningful engagement and trust-building. Agencies should track a combination of quantitative and qualitative metrics.

1. Engagement Metrics

- **Likes, Shares, and Comments:** Measures how much the public interacts with content.
- **Replies and Conversations:** Tracks how often the agency engages in two-way discussions.

2. Reach and Visibility

- **Follower Growth:** Monitors audience expansion over time.
- **Impressions and Views:** Measures how many people see agency posts.
- **Website Clicks:** Tracks traffic generated from social media to official agency pages.

3. Crisis and Emergency Response Metrics

- **Speed of Updates:** Evaluates how quickly critical information is posted.
- **Public Reaction and Compliance:** Measures how effectively emergency messages prompt action.
- **Misinformation Correction:** Tracks how well false information is countered and corrected.

4. Community Sentiment Analysis

- **Positive vs. Negative Mentions:** Helps gauge public perception.
- **Recurring Themes in Feedback:** Identifies common concerns or areas of praise.
- **Surveys and Polls:** Directly collects public input on agency performance.

Tools for Measuring Social Media Performance

There are numerous tools available to help law enforcement agencies track performance and analyze data.

Recommended Tools:

- **Native Platform Insights** (Facebook Insights, Twitter/X Analytics, Instagram Insights)
- **Google Analytics** (Tracks website traffic from social media posts)
- **Social Media Management Platforms** (Hootsuite, Sprout Social, Buffer)
- **Sentiment Analysis Tools** (Brandwatch, Meltwater, Talkwalker)

Adjusting Strategy Based on Data

1. Identify High-Performing Content

   - Determine which posts get the most engagement and replicate their success.
   - Analyze post timing, format, and messaging for effectiveness.

2. Improve Underperforming Areas

   - If engagement is low, adjust posting frequency, visuals, or tone.
   - Test different content styles (e.g., videos, infographics, live updates).

3. Enhance Community Interaction

- Increase responsiveness to comments and questions.
- Experiment with more interactive posts (polls, Q&A sessions, live chats).

4. Refine Emergency Communication

- Review past crisis response effectiveness.
- Develop templates for faster, more effective emergency messaging.

Regular Audits and Strategy Reviews

Conducting periodic social media audits ensures agencies stay on track and adapt to changing public needs.

Steps for a Social Media Audit:

1. **Review Metrics Quarterly** – Compare data over time to track trends.
2. **Assess Goal Achievement** – Determine if objectives are being met or need adjustments.
3. **Gather Team Feedback** – Get insights from those managing social media accounts.
4. **Update Content Plans** – Refine posting schedules, themes, and messaging as needed.

For a help with a social media audit, use the worksheet in *Appendix B: Social Media Worksheets*

The Road Ahead

Measuring success isn't just about numbers—it's about ensuring social media efforts align with agency goals and community needs. By regularly evaluating performance and making data-driven adjustments, law enforcement agencies can strengthen public trust and maximize the impact of their digital presence.

In the next chapter, we'll explore the evolving landscape of **social media ethics and digital security**, ensuring agencies maintain credibility while protecting sensitive information.

Social Media Ethics

The Importance of Ethics in Law Enforcement Social Media

Law enforcement agencies operate in a highly visible space, making ethical considerations crucial in social media communication. Every post, comment, and interaction must reflect professionalism, integrity, and transparency to maintain public trust.

Key Ethical Considerations:
- **Accuracy and Truthfulness** – Ensure all shared information is verified and factual to avoid spreading misinformation.
- **Respect for Privacy** – Avoid sharing personally identifiable information (PII) without consent.
- **Impartiality** – Maintain a neutral and unbiased tone, avoiding political or controversial statements.
- **Transparency** – Clearly communicate agency policies and updates while being open about mistakes when they occur.
- **Respectful Engagement** – Uphold professionalism in responses, even when dealing with criticism.

Handling Sensitive Information Responsibly

Law enforcement social media must balance public transparency with operational security. Certain details should not be shared online to protect individuals and investigations.

Do Not Share:

- Personal details of victims, witnesses, or suspects.
- Tactical law enforcement strategies.
- Unverified crime reports or speculative information.
- Internal memos or confidential communications.

Guidelines for Sharing Crime-Related Information:

- Only release confirmed details.
- Ensure posts comply with legal requirements and privacy laws.
- When in doubt, consult legal advisors before posting sensitive updates.

Addressing Ethical Dilemmas in Social Media

Even with guidelines in place, ethical challenges can arise. Agencies must be prepared to handle difficult situations professionally and with integrity.

Examples of Ethical Dilemmas:

- **Handling Negative Comments** – Should an agency respond, ignore, or delete inflammatory remarks?
- **Use of Surveillance on Social Media** – What are the boundaries for monitoring public posts?
- **Off-Duty Social Media Activity** – Should agencies regulate personal accounts of officers?
- **Breaking News Situations** – How much information should be shared, and when?

Recommended Approaches:

- Develop a clear decision-making framework for ethical dilemmas.
- Provide training to officers and social media managers on ethical considerations.
- Be transparent when mistakes occur and outline steps taken to correct them.

The Road Ahead

As technology and public expectations evolve, so must law enforcement's approach to social media ethics. By prioritizing responsible digital communication and strong security practices, agencies can foster trust and protect their online presence.

Risk Management and Digital Integrity

Introduction

Social media is a powerful tool for law enforcement, enabling real-time communication, community engagement, and crisis response. However, it also presents risks, including misinformation, public backlash, and account security threats. Agencies must proactively manage these risks to maintain public trust and ensure responsible digital communication.

1. Identifying and Managing Misinformation

Misinformation can spread quickly on social media, potentially undermining public confidence and law enforcement operations.

Best Practices:

- **Monitor for False Information:** Use social listening tools to detect and track misinformation trends.
- **Respond Promptly and Factually:** Address misinformation directly with verified facts and official statements.
- **Pin Verified Information:** Keep critical updates visible by pinning posts on platforms like Facebook and Twitter.
- **Engage Trusted Community Partners:** Collaborate with local media, government agencies, and community leaders to amplify accurate messaging.
- **Use Visual Fact-Checking Methods:** Share infographics and videos that debunk myths quickly and effectively.

2. Handling Inappropriate Content and Public Backlash

Law enforcement agencies may encounter negative comments, online harassment, or controversial discussions on social media.

Best Practices:

- **Develop a Comment Moderation Policy:** Outline what constitutes acceptable public discourse and enforce it consistently.
- **Avoid Engaging in Arguments:** Maintain professionalism and avoid public disputes.
- **Encourage Constructive Dialogue:** Redirect controversial discussions toward solutions and facts.
- **Remove Harmful or Threatening Content:** Follow platform guidelines for reporting and removing comments that promote violence or misinformation.
- **Respond with Empathy and Authority:** Address community concerns while reinforcing agency integrity.

3. Protecting Social Media Accounts from Unauthorized Use

While Chapter 8 covers cybersecurity in depth, agencies should still implement key account protection strategies for social media platforms.

Best Practices:

- **Limit Account Access:** Only authorized personnel should have credentials for official accounts.
- **Use Role-Based Permissions:** Assign different access levels based on responsibilities.
- **Conduct Regular Access Audits:** Remove former employees and inactive accounts promptly.
- **Enable Account Recovery Options:** Set up backup emails and authentication steps to regain access in case of an issue.
- **Monitor Login Activity:** Track unauthorized attempts and unusual login locations.

For detailed cybersecurity measures, refer to
Chapter 8: Cybersecurity Best Practices.

Crisis Communication on Social Media

Law enforcement agencies must be prepared to communicate effectively during crises, ensuring that the public receives accurate, timely, and actionable information. The following best practices should guide emergency messaging:

- Be the **first verified source of information** to prevent misinformation from spreading.

- **Use pinned posts** on platforms like Facebook and Twitter/X for high-priority alerts.

- **Prioritize accuracy over speed**—if details are still unfolding, acknowledge that.

Pre-Written Crisis Response Templates

Breaking Emergency (Active Threat/Shooter)
"We are responding to an active incident in [location]. Please avoid the area and follow official updates here. More details will be shared as they become available."

Traffic Disruption
"Road closures are in effect due to [incident]. Please use alternative routes. Updates will follow."

Rumor Control / Misinformation Correction
"Misinformation is spreading regarding [incident]. Here are the verified facts: [Insert Link]. Always check with official sources before sharing unverified claims."

Ongoing Investigation
"We are actively investigating [incident] and will share updates as soon as possible. If you have information, please contact [number]."

Incident Resolved / Public Reassurance
"The situation at [location] is now resolved. Law enforcement remains on scene for public safety. Thank you for your cooperation."

Best Practices for Live-streaming During a Crisis

In addition to written updates, agencies should consider **Facebook Live, YouTube Live, or Instagram Stories** to provide real-time updates. Livestreams should be used for:

- **Press conferences and briefings**

- **Public safety announcements**

- **Addressing misinformation in real-time**

Conclusion

Managing social media risks requires a proactive strategy that balances transparency, security, and public engagement. By effectively addressing misinformation, handling online interactions professionally, securing accounts, and preparing for crisis communications, law enforcement agencies can strengthen digital integrity and public trust.

Cybersecurity Best Practices

Introduction

As law enforcement agencies increasingly rely on digital platforms, the risk of cyber threats continues to rise. Cybersecurity breaches can compromise sensitive information, spread misinformation, and damage public trust. This chapter provides a structured approach to safeguarding digital assets, ensuring the integrity of official communications, and maintaining operational security.

1. Strengthening Account Security

Law enforcement social media accounts and digital tools must be secured against unauthorized access to prevent cyber intrusions.

Best Practices:

- Enable **Multi-Factor Authentication (MFA)** on all social media accounts to require an extra layer of verification beyond just a password.
- Limit **administrative access** to trained personnel only, ensuring role-based permissions to prevent unauthorized modifications.
- Use **strong, unique passwords** and update them regularly, storing them in a secure password manager.
- Conduct **regular access audits**, immediately revoking access for former employees or personnel who no longer require account permissions.

2. Monitoring for Threats and Unauthorized Activity

Continuous monitoring is essential to detect and mitigate cybersecurity threats before they escalate into major security incidents.

Best Practices:

- Monitor for **fake accounts and impersonation attempts**, reporting fraudulent profiles to social media platforms for removal.
- Implement **AI-driven threat detection** to identify unusual patterns, unauthorized login attempts, or bot-driven disinformation campaigns.
- Set up **alerts and notifications** for suspicious account activity.
- Establish **real-time monitoring** with social listening tools to detect potential security threats or misinformation campaigns early.

3. Secure Devices and Network Usage

Ensuring that devices and network connections used for digital communication are secure can prevent cyberattacks from infiltrating agency systems.

Best Practices:

- Use **agency-approved devices** for social media management and official communication.
- Require staff to connect through a **VPN (Virtual Private Network)** when accessing accounts remotely to encrypt sensitive data.
- Avoid logging into official accounts on **public or unsecured Wi-Fi networks**, which can expose credentials to cybercriminals.
- Regularly update and install **antivirus and anti-malware software** on all devices.
- Enable **remote device wipe capabilities** to protect sensitive data in case of lost or stolen devices.

4. Preventing Phishing and Social Engineering Attacks

Phishing and social engineering attacks are commonly used to trick employees into revealing confidential information. Agencies must train personnel to recognize these threats.

Best Practices:

- Conduct **regular phishing awareness training** to educate employees on identifying phishing emails and suspicious links.
- Implement **employee phishing simulations** to test and improve awareness.
- Verify **unexpected login requests** or password resets through a separate communication channel.
- Never click on **suspicious links or attachments** in unsolicited messages.
- Require verification for **any sensitive data requests** from external sources.

5. Crisis Response and Recovery Planning

Despite preventive measures, cyber incidents can still occur. Having a well-defined crisis response plan ensures agencies can act swiftly in case of security breaches.

Best Practices:

- Develop a **cybersecurity incident response plan**, outlining step-by-step actions to take in the event of a cyberattack or data breach.
- Prepare **pre-drafted public statements** to maintain transparency and public trust during security incidents.
- Establish a **backup communication channel** to use if primary accounts are compromised.
- Assign a **cybersecurity liaison** to coordinate with IT specialists and law enforcement cyber units.
- Conduct **regular cybersecurity drills** to test response readiness and improve preparedness.

6. Managing Multi-Factor Authentication (MFA) Codes Securely

Multi-factor authentication (MFA) is an essential security measure for protecting agency social media accounts. However, social media teams often face challenges in securely sharing MFA codes when multiple users need access. To prevent unauthorized access while ensuring operational efficiency, agencies must establish best practices for managing MFA credentials.

Secure Methods for Sharing MFA Codes

1. **Use a Dedicated Authentication App:**

   - Agencies should use authentication apps such as **Google Authenticator, Microsoft Authenticator, or Duo Security** instead of SMS-based authentication, which is more vulnerable to interception.

   - These apps generate time-sensitive codes that can be accessed only by authorized personnel.

2. **Centralized MFA Management via Password Managers:**

   - Agencies can use secure password managers like **1Password, LastPass, or Bitwarden** to store and share MFA backup codes among authorized personnel.

   - Password managers allow role-based access control, ensuring only approved users can retrieve MFA credentials when needed.

3. **Dedicated Agency Device for MFA Access:**

   - Assign a **secure department-issued device** (e.g., a tablet or secondary phone) to store and retrieve MFA codes.

   - Limit access to this device to essential personnel, such as the Public Information Officer (PIO) and IT security team.

4. **MFA Code Retrieval Workflow:** To ensure security, agencies should follow a structured workflow for accessing MFA codes when needed.

MFA Code Retrieval Workflow

Step	Action
1. Access Request	A team member needing MFA access submits a request to the designated account administrator (e.g., PIO or IT security).
2. Verification	The administrator verifies the requestor's identity using pre-established authentication protocols.
3. Code Retrieval	The administrator retrieves the MFA code securely via the authentication app or password manager.
4. Secure Delivery	The code is shared via an encrypted messaging app (e.g., Signal) or directly communicated through a secure internal channel.
5. Confirmation	The requestor confirms access, and the administrator logs the request for auditing purposes.

Additional Best Practices for Secure MFA Management

- **Limit the Number of MFA-Authorized Users:** Only essential personnel should have access to MFA credentials to reduce security risks.

- **Enable Role-Based Access Control (RBAC):** Restrict social media account access based on job roles, ensuring only designated individuals can retrieve login credentials.

- **Regularly Rotate Backup Codes:** Many authentication apps allow agencies to regenerate backup codes periodically. This prevents unauthorized access in case a previous code is compromised.

- **Log and Monitor MFA Access Requests:** Agencies should keep records of who accesses MFA credentials and when, ensuring accountability and security.

- **Have an Emergency Access Plan:** If the primary MFA holder is unavailable, agencies should have a backup administrator who can securely access and share authentication credentials.

By implementing these MFA management strategies, agencies can enhance cybersecurity while maintaining operational efficiency for their social media teams.

Conclusion

As cyber threats evolve, law enforcement agencies must remain vigilant and proactive in protecting their digital presence. Implementing strong security measures, training personnel, and developing a crisis response plan can help agencies safeguard their online communications and maintain public trust. Cybersecurity is not a one-time effort—it requires continuous adaptation and improvement to stay ahead of emerging threats.

ADA Compliance in Social Media

Introduction

Ensuring accessibility in law enforcement social media communications is not just a best practice—it is a legal obligation. The Americans with Disabilities Act (ADA) requires that digital communication be accessible to all individuals, including those with disabilities. With the **new Department of Justice (DOJ) ADA rules** set to take effect in **2026**, agencies must proactively adapt their digital strategies to comply with these updated regulations. This chapter provides a comprehensive guide to ADA compliance in law enforcement social media, covering essential accessibility requirements, practical implementation steps, and the legal implications of non-compliance.

1. Understanding ADA Compliance for Digital Content

The ADA mandates that digital platforms, including government social media accounts, must be accessible to people with disabilities. This includes individuals with visual, auditory, motor, and cognitive impairments. The Web Content Accessibility Guidelines (WCAG) provide the gold standard for achieving digital accessibility.

Key ADA and WCAG 2.1 Guidelines for Social Media

- **Alternative Text (Alt Text):** All images must include descriptive alt text to ensure screen readers can convey the image's content to visually impaired users. For example, instead of writing "officer speaking," use "Police Chief Smith speaking at a community event about public safety initiatives."
- **Captioning for Videos:** All video content must include accurate captions to provide access for individuals who are deaf or hard of hearing. Automated captions should always be reviewed and edited

for accuracy. Agencies can use tools like YouTube's caption editor or third-party software to ensure proper synchronization.

- **Readable Fonts and Contrast Ratios:** Text must have sufficient contrast with the background and use easy-to-read fonts. White text on a bright yellow background, for example, can be difficult to read. High-contrast colors like black on white or dark blue on light gray are preferred.
- **Keyboard Navigation:** Social media content should be navigable using only a keyboard for those with motor disabilities. This means ensuring that users can tab through links and interactive elements without requiring a mouse.
- **Plain Language Communication:** Posts should use clear, straightforward language to accommodate users with cognitive disabilities. Instead of "Ensure compliance with mandated procedural obligations," use "Follow the required steps to meet legal rules."

2. Overview of the 2026 DOJ ADA Rules

In 2026, new DOJ rules will expand ADA enforcement to explicitly cover digital content, including social media and websites for government agencies. Key requirements include:

- **Mandatory WCAG 2.1 AA Compliance:** Law enforcement agencies must meet WCAG 2.1 AA standards for digital content. This means ensuring that all online communications are accessible, including website updates, social media posts, and shared documents.
- **Timely Accessibility Updates:** Agencies must ensure all new digital content, including social media posts, is accessible at the time of publication. Delayed updates will not be considered compliant.
- **Public Complaint Mechanism:** Agencies must implement a process for individuals to report accessibility issues and request accommodations. This could include an accessibility hotline, email contact, or a dedicated website page for reporting concerns.
- **Enforcement and Penalties:** The DOJ will have increased enforcement capabilities, with potential legal and financial penalties

for non-compliance. Agencies should establish internal compliance teams to audit digital accessibility regularly.

3. Best Practices for Ensuring ADA Compliance on Social Media

Image Accessibility

- Always include **alt text** when posting images on social media. This is particularly important for infographics, maps, and photos that provide critical information.
- Use **descriptive language** rather than vague terms like "image of a police officer." Instead, describe the action or context, such as "Officer Jane Doe assisting a resident at a community safety fair."
- Avoid text-heavy images that lack readable alternative formats. If an image contains text, provide the full written content in the post's caption or link to a webpage with the same information.

Video Accessibility

- Enable **automatic captions** on platforms like YouTube and Facebook, but always review and correct errors. AI-generated captions are often inaccurate and can misrepresent important details.
- Provide **transcripts** for videos and livestream events. These should be available on the department's website or as downloadable PDFs.
- Ensure that videos do not contain flashing elements that could trigger seizures. If necessary, include a warning before such content.

Text & Formatting Accessibility

- Use **CamelCase hashtags** (e.g., #LawEnforcementNews instead of #lawenforcementnews) to improve readability for screen readers.

- Avoid **all caps** in posts, as screen readers may misinterpret them as abbreviations or read them in a distorted tone.
- Ensure **hyperlinks** are descriptive. Instead of "Click here," use "Learn more about our community safety program."

Livestream Accessibility

- Provide **real-time captions** for all livestreams. Platforms like Zoom and Microsoft Teams offer live captioning features.
- Announce when **ASL interpreters** are available for press conferences or town halls. This information should be included in event promotions.
- Offer **multiple ways to access content**, such as simultaneous text-based updates on agency websites or social media posts summarizing key points from a livestream.

Keyboard & Navigation Considerations

- Ensure that interactive social media features, such as polls and comment sections, are keyboard-navigable.
- Use **simplified language** and avoid jargon-heavy content to ensure messages are easily understood by a diverse audience.

4. Implementation Strategy for Law Enforcement Agencies

Step 1: Conduct an Accessibility Audit

- Review current social media content and platforms for ADA compliance gaps.
- Use accessibility checkers and screen readers to test content usability. Common tools include WAVE (Web Accessibility Evaluation Tool) and the NVDA screen reader.

Step 2: Train Social Media Teams on ADA Standards

- Educate personnel on WCAG guidelines and the 2026 DOJ requirements.
- Implement internal accessibility checklists for all posts.
- Provide annual refresher training for all team members.

Step 3: Establish an Accessibility Policy and Reporting System

- Create a publicly available accessibility policy that outlines the agency's commitment to inclusive digital communication.
- Provide a designated contact for accessibility complaints and accommodation requests.

Step 4: Regularly Update and Monitor Compliance

- Schedule quarterly accessibility reviews with a dedicated compliance officer or team.
- Adapt to evolving social media platform accessibility features and legal updates.

5. Legal and Reputational Risks of Non-Compliance

Failure to comply with ADA requirements and the new DOJ rules can result in:

- **Legal Consequences:** Lawsuits, DOJ enforcement actions, and financial penalties.
- **Reputational Damage:** Public backlash for failing to provide equal access to digital information.
- **Operational Challenges:** Inaccessible content limits public engagement and weakens community trust.

Conclusion

Law enforcement agencies must prioritize ADA compliance in social media communications to ensure accessibility, transparency, and legal adherence. The **2026 DOJ ADA rules** underscore the necessity of implementing accessibility measures now to avoid future penalties. By adopting best practices and staying proactive, agencies can foster inclusivity and improve public trust in digital engagement.

Training and Capacity Building

The Need for Social Media Training in Law Enforcement

Effective social media use requires more than just an account and a posting schedule—it demands training, strategy, and consistency. Law enforcement personnel must be equipped with the skills necessary to manage digital communication professionally, ethically, and efficiently.

Key Objectives of Training:

1. **Ensure Consistency** – All posts and interactions should align with agency policies and messaging. A lack of consistency in tone and messaging can lead to confusion and undermine public trust. Training ensures that all personnel understand and follow the same communication guidelines.
2. **Maintain Professionalism** – Officers and staff should know how to engage with the public respectfully and effectively. Professional communication fosters positive relationships with the community and ensures that all interactions reflect well on the department.
3. **Enhance Crisis Preparedness** – Training prepares personnel for managing social media during emergencies. Without proper preparation, agencies risk spreading misinformation or failing to provide timely updates, which can lead to panic and distrust.
4. **Prevent Security Breaches** – Educating staff on cybersecurity measures reduces risks of hacking or misinformation. Unauthorized access to an agency's social media accounts can result in significant reputational damage and loss of credibility.
5. **Improve Community Engagement** – Learning best practices helps foster trust and transparency. When agencies engage effectively, they can create a sense of partnership with the public and encourage constructive dialogue.

Core Components of a Law Enforcement Social Media Training Program

1. Platform-Specific Training

Each social media platform has unique functions, audiences, and best practices. Training should focus on understanding how to effectively use Twitter/X for real-time updates, Facebook for community discussions, Instagram and TikTok for visual storytelling, and LinkedIn for professional networking. Personnel should also be trained on adapting content to suit each platform's strengths and audience expectations.

2. Crisis Communication Readiness

Agencies must be prepared to handle crisis situations with speed and accuracy. Simulated emergency drills can help staff practice responding to different scenarios, ensuring they are ready when real situations arise. Developing pre-approved messaging templates can also help agencies provide timely, consistent updates without delays.

3. Legal and Ethical Considerations

Social media posts from law enforcement agencies are often subject to legal scrutiny. Training should include education on First Amendment rights, public records laws, and privacy regulations to ensure that all content adheres to legal guidelines. Officers should also understand the ethical implications of sharing certain information and the importance of avoiding biased or inappropriate content.

4. Security and Cyber Awareness

Social media accounts can be vulnerable to hacking, phishing attacks, and impersonation attempts. Agencies should implement strong password protocols, multi-factor authentication, and regular security audits to prevent breaches. Personnel must be trained to recognize cybersecurity threats and take appropriate action to protect the agency's digital presence.

5. Content Creation and Storytelling

Engaging content is crucial for maintaining public interest and fostering trust. Training should cover how to craft clear, concise, and engaging posts, as well as best practices for using photos, videos, and graphics to enhance storytelling. Officers should be encouraged to highlight positive community interactions and share information in a way that resonates with the audience.

6. Handling Public Interaction and Criticism

Public engagement on social media can sometimes be challenging, particularly when agencies face criticism or controversy. Personnel must be trained on how to respond to questions, address concerns, and de-escalate tense conversations. Agencies should establish clear guidelines for when to engage, when to ignore, and when to escalate issues for further review.

Ongoing Education and Policy Updates

Social media evolves rapidly, and training should be an ongoing process rather than a one-time event. Agencies must stay up to date with new technologies, policy changes, and evolving public expectations.

Steps for Continuous Learning:

1. **Regular Training Workshops** – Hold quarterly training sessions to keep staff up to date. These workshops can focus on platform updates, emerging best practices, and lessons learned from recent events.

2. **Policy Reviews** – Regularly update guidelines to reflect new laws and platform policies. Social media policies should be reviewed annually to ensure they remain relevant and effective.
3. **Cross-Agency Collaboration** – Learn from best practices and case studies from other departments. Sharing insights with other law enforcement agencies can help refine strategies and improve overall effectiveness.
4. **Performance Audits** – Evaluate social media effectiveness and adjust strategies accordingly. Regularly analyzing engagement metrics and feedback helps identify areas for improvement and ensures that goals are being met.

Officer Social Media Conduct and Best Practices

Law enforcement officers' social media use, both on and off duty, can have a significant impact on public trust and departmental credibility. Agencies should provide clear guidelines to ensure professionalism, privacy protection, and legal compliance.

Best Practices for Officer Social Media Use

Do:

- Adjust privacy settings on personal accounts.

- Use discretion before posting.

- Fact-check before reposting law enforcement-related content.

- Report impersonation attempts of your account.

Don't:

- Share sensitive case details online.

- Engage in political debates or controversial topics.

- Post offensive, discriminatory, or inflammatory content.

- Engage in arguments or hostile exchanges online.

Disciplinary Action Policy

To ensure accountability, agencies should implement a **tiered disciplinary system** for social media violations:

- **Minor Violations**: First offense – Verbal warning and policy review.

- **Major Violations**: (e.g., sharing investigation details) – Suspension of social media privileges.

- **Severe Violations**: (e.g., hate speech, leaking confidential data) – Disciplinary action, possible termination.

Encouraging Positive Social Media Use

While officers must adhere to professional guidelines, agencies should also encourage positive engagement on social media. Law enforcement personnel can use social media to:

- Share **community service stories**.

- Promote **recruitment and public outreach**.

- Support **crime prevention education and awareness campaigns**.

Providing officers with **ongoing social media training** and clearly defined policies ensures that their online presence aligns with agency values and public expectations. Refer to **Appendix G: Officer Social Media Training Framework** for additional guidance on implementing structured training programs.

Final Thoughts

As social media becomes an essential tool for law enforcement, agencies must invest in ongoing training to ensure their teams are equipped with the latest strategies and technologies. A well-trained staff is the foundation of a credible and responsive digital presence. By committing to continuous learning, agencies can enhance engagement, improve crisis response, and maintain public trust in an evolving digital landscape.

Future Trends in Social Media

The Evolving Digital Landscape

The way law enforcement agencies use social media today will look very different in the years to come. As technology advances, public expectations shift, and new challenges emerge, agencies must stay ahead of trends to remain effective in their digital communication efforts.

Key Areas of Change:

1. **Rise of AI and Automation** – Artificial intelligence will play a larger role in content creation, moderation, and engagement. AI-generated text and image tools can assist agencies in crafting more engaging posts while reducing workload. However, agencies must also remain vigilant against AI-generated misinformation, which can be used to manipulate public perception or spread false narratives.

2. **Increased Public Demand for Transparency** – Agencies will need to be more proactive in sharing information and addressing public concerns. With growing calls for accountability in law enforcement, social media will serve as a direct line of communication where agencies can showcase transparency through regular updates, case progress reports, and community engagement efforts.

3. **Growth of Private and Encrypted Platforms** – With more conversations moving to private groups and encrypted messaging apps, law enforcement will need new strategies for engagement. Traditional social media platforms may no longer be the primary space where critical discussions occur, requiring agencies to find alternative ways to communicate with their communities while respecting privacy and ethical considerations.

4. **Greater Use of Video and Live Streaming** – Short-form video content and live updates will become even more essential for public trust and engagement. Agencies will need to invest in training

personnel on best practices for video storytelling, ensuring messages are clear, concise, and visually compelling.

5. **Cybersecurity and Deepfake Threats** – Agencies must prepare for the growing risk of AI-generated misinformation and impersonation attacks. Deepfake technology is becoming more sophisticated, allowing bad actors to create highly realistic but false depictions of events. Law enforcement agencies must develop tools and partnerships to quickly detect, verify, and counteract such threats before they spread widely.

The Impact of Artificial Intelligence and Automation

AI-Powered Content Creation

- AI tools can assist in generating social media posts, captions, and alerts, helping agencies maintain a consistent presence. With AI, agencies can quickly generate informative posts, summarize reports, and tailor content to different platforms efficiently. However, it's critical to review AI-generated content for accuracy and tone to maintain public trust.
- Chatbots may handle basic inquiries, freeing up human personnel for more complex engagements. Automated responses can assist in answering frequently asked questions, such as reporting crime tips, office hours, or safety guidelines, while still directing critical issues to human responders.

AI for Monitoring and Misinformation Detection

- Automated tools can scan social media for emerging crises, misinformation, and public sentiment. AI-powered social listening tools can help agencies track trends, detect potential threats, and assess public perception in real time, enabling them to react faster and more strategically.
- AI-assisted moderation can help agencies detect and address harmful or misleading content more efficiently. By filtering out

inappropriate content and detecting misleading claims, AI can help ensure that agency social media pages remain credible and constructive environments for public discussion.

Transparency and Public Trust

Demand for Real-Time Updates

- The public expects faster, more transparent communication. Agencies will need to use real-time data-sharing tools to keep community members informed. This includes dashboards, live-streamed press conferences, and detailed case progress updates to reduce speculation and misinformation.
- Dashboards and interactive data visualizations can provide insights on crime trends, policing efforts, and community outreach programs. By offering easy-to-understand statistics and visual representations of data, agencies can improve public understanding and confidence in law enforcement activities.

Ethical Challenges of Digital Transparency

- Agencies must balance the need for transparency with privacy concerns and legal limitations. Oversharing details about ongoing investigations or releasing sensitive information can jeopardize cases, requiring agencies to develop clear policies on what can be shared and when.
- Clear policies must be in place to ensure responsible sharing of digital information. Agencies should develop guidelines to determine appropriate levels of disclosure while safeguarding individual rights and upholding legal requirements.

The Shift to Private and Encrypted Platforms

Engaging on Community-Based Apps

- Apps like Nextdoor and WhatsApp are becoming key spaces for community discussion and safety updates. These platforms allow agencies to reach local audiences with hyper-targeted messages, but they also require tailored communication strategies to ensure messages are relevant and effective.
- Agencies must develop strategies for providing official information while respecting platform limitations. Unlike traditional social media, these platforms often have stricter moderation rules and user privacy controls that agencies must navigate carefully.

Challenges of Monitoring Encrypted Conversations

- Encrypted messaging services like Signal and Telegram limit agencies' ability to track criminal activity. While privacy protections are crucial for personal freedoms, they can also hinder law enforcement efforts to monitor criminal communications. Agencies must find a balance between respecting privacy rights and ensuring public safety.
- Partnerships with tech companies may help law enforcement navigate these challenges responsibly. Collaboration with technology providers can help agencies access critical information while maintaining ethical oversight and public accountability.

The Dominance of Video and Live-streaming

The Continued Rise of Short-Form Video

- TikTok, Instagram Reels, and YouTube Shorts will continue to shape public engagement. Agencies that adopt short-form video formats effectively can reach a wider audience, making public safety messages more accessible and impactful.

- Agencies must master storytelling through video while maintaining professionalism and credibility. Training personnel on video best practices, scripting, and production quality will be crucial in ensuring effective communication.

Live Streaming for Crisis Communication

- Real-time video updates can be powerful tools during emergencies, but agencies must train personnel to handle live broadcasts effectively. Live updates require careful planning, as they involve rapid information sharing with little room for error.
- Engaging with the public through Q&A sessions or town hall-style discussions can strengthen community relationships. Offering interactive sessions where community members can ask questions fosters transparency and builds trust between law enforcement and the public.

Preparing for Deepfake and Cybersecurity Threats

The Threat of AI-Generated Misinformation

- Deepfake videos and altered images can be used to spread false narratives about law enforcement. Agencies must stay ahead by investing in digital forensics tools that can detect manipulated content and disprove false claims before they gain traction.
- Agencies must develop strategies to verify authenticity and quickly debunk false information. Rapid response teams should be established to assess digital threats and issue factual corrections through official channels.

Strengthening Cybersecurity Measures

- Implementing robust authentication protocols can help prevent hacking and account takeovers. Agencies must enforce strict security measures such as multi-factor authentication and encrypted communications to safeguard their digital presence.
- Training personnel to recognize cyber threats and phishing attempts will be crucial in maintaining digital security. Employees should receive regular training on recognizing cyber threats and responding appropriately to prevent data breaches.

Future-Proofing Strategies for Law Enforcement Social Media

To remain relevant and effective in the evolving digital landscape, law enforcement agencies must take a **proactive approach** to future challenges. The following strategies will help agencies anticipate changes and build resilience into their social media operations.

Invest in Digital Literacy and AI Awareness

- Train officers and social media personnel on emerging technologies, including AI-driven misinformation and digital forensic tools.

- Regularly update crisis communication plans to include deepfake verification protocols.

Build Flexible Social Media Policies

- Ensure policies are adaptable to emerging platforms and evolving public expectations.

- Establish clear guidelines on the ethical use of AI tools in content creation and moderation.

- Regularly review and update best practices for handling misinformation, privacy concerns, and community engagement.

Strengthen Multi-Platform Communication Strategies

- Expand agency presence beyond traditional platforms to include emerging networks and community-based apps.

- Maintain a consistent voice across multiple platforms while tailoring content to each audience's preferences.

- Use alternative communication channels, such as encrypted messaging apps, for verified public safety updates.

Regularly Audit and Adapt Social Media Strategies

- Conduct quarterly reviews of engagement metrics, misinformation trends, and public sentiment analysis.

- Experiment with new content formats, such as interactive AR/VR experiences for public education.

- Stay informed on legislative changes that impact digital communication and law enforcement transparency.

Emerging Social Media Platforms

As part of adapting to future trends, agencies must be aware of **new and evolving social media platforms** that could shape community engagement. While platforms like Facebook, Twitter/X, and TikTok remain dominant, newer alternatives are gaining traction.

Notable Emerging Platforms:

- **Threads (Meta)** – A text-based alternative to Twitter/X, designed for public discourse and integrated with Instagram.

- **Bluesky** – A decentralized platform offering user-controlled content moderation and algorithmic flexibility.

- **Mastodon** – A non-algorithmic, open-source platform that allows agencies to join different "instances" to engage with hyper-specific audiences.

- **Discord** – Originally for gamers, now widely used for community-based discussions with private and public servers.

- **BeReal** – A platform promoting authenticity through spontaneous, unedited photo sharing.

For a deeper look at these and other **emerging social media platforms**, see **Appendix D: Overview of Emerging Social Media Platforms**.

The Future of Law Enforcement Social Media

Social media's role in law enforcement will only continue to evolve. Agencies must remain adaptive, transparent, and innovative to foster public trust and engagement.

Future Trends to Watch:

- **AI-powered chatbots** for answering FAQs and redirecting non-emergency reports.

- **Augmented Reality (AR) & Virtual Reality (VR)** for crime prevention education.

- **Increased use of live-streaming** for town halls and real-time event coverage.

- **Greater integration with community-driven apps** like Nextdoor for neighborhood-specific updates.

Looking Ahead

The digital landscape is shifting rapidly, with new platforms, AI advancements, and misinformation challenges reshaping public engagement. Law enforcement agencies must stay agile, exploring emerging technologies while upholding ethical standards and community trust. By anticipating changes and adopting proactive strategies, agencies can remain at the forefront of digital communication, fostering stronger relationships with their communities.

Building a Digital Trust & Engagement

Moving Beyond Daily Posting to a Long-Term Public Trust Strategy

In the digital age, law enforcement agencies can no longer rely solely on traditional media or periodic updates to build trust with their communities. Social media has become an essential tool for transparency, engagement, and long-term relationship-building. To truly gain and maintain public trust, agencies must develop a sustained digital trust strategy that goes beyond daily posting and viral content.

Creating a Professionalism & Transparency Plan for Social Media

To build and maintain digital trust, agencies must have a clear and structured approach to professionalism and transparency in their social media practices. This plan should align with organizational values, ethical standards, and community expectations.

Steps to Implement a Professionalism & Transparency Plan:

Define the Agency's Digital Identity

- Establish a social media voice that is professional, informative, and approachable.
- Maintain consistency across all platforms to ensure credibility.
- Avoid forced trends that may seem disingenuous.

Commit to Open and Honest Communication

- Share both successes and challenges with the public.

- Provide regular insights into department activities and operations.
- Address difficult topics proactively rather than waiting for public criticism.

Implement a Clear and Fair Commenting Policy

- Allow constructive discussions while setting boundaries to prevent harassment and misinformation.
- Moderate comments transparently, ensuring that deletions or restrictions are based on clear policy guidelines.
- Encourage public participation while maintaining respectful discourse.

Develop and Follow Crisis Communication Guidelines

- Be the first and most reliable source of information in emergency situations.
- Avoid speculation and focus on facts, providing real-time updates when possible.
- Engage with the public to address concerns while reinforcing trust through accuracy.

Use Data and Feedback to Improve Public Relations

- Monitor audience sentiment and engagement metrics to assess trust levels.
- Conduct surveys or polls to gather public input on law enforcement issues.
- Adapt social media strategies based on community feedback and emerging challenges.

Ensure Leadership Engagement in Digital Trust Efforts

- Encourage agency leadership to take an active role in online conversations.
- Feature department heads in video messages or live Q&A sessions to humanize the agency.
- Reinforce internal training on ethical digital engagement and social media professionalism.

Adapting Best Practices to Fit Your Agency

Every law enforcement agency has different challenges, community needs, and available resources. Here's how to apply successful social media strategies in a way that fits **your specific agency**:

1. Start with a Focused Approach

- Instead of trying to be on **every** social media platform, prioritize the ones most used by your community.
- **Example:** If your city has an active Facebook audience, start by making that your **primary engagement hub**.

2. Customize Content for Local Concerns

- Pay attention to **community-specific issues** and create content around those topics.
- **Example:** If auto theft is rising in your area, launch an **Instagram series on car theft prevention** with real case studies.

3. Empower Officers to Be Digital Ambassadors

- Select officers who are **comfortable on camera** to represent the agency online.
- **Example:** Assign school resource officers to run **TikTok safety challenges** for local high school students.

4. Invest in Training & Cybersecurity

- Train staff to **handle criticism professionally**, **verify information**, and **secure accounts against cyber threats**.
- **Example:** If your department experiences misinformation, be ready with **pre-approved response templates**.

The Path Forward

Trust and engagement are built through consistency, transparency, and meaningful interactions. Law enforcement agencies that prioritize authentic communication and public responsiveness will strengthen their relationships with the communities they serve. By fostering open dialogue, addressing concerns with professionalism, and leveraging social media effectively, agencies can create a long-term foundation of public confidence and cooperation.

Engaging Younger Audiences

The Challenge of Reaching Younger Audiences

Younger generations, particularly Gen Z and Millennials, consume and interact with social media differently than older demographics. They value authenticity, relatability, and engagement over formal institutional messaging. For law enforcement agencies, the challenge is finding ways to communicate effectively without appearing forced, outdated, or insincere.

Dos and Don'ts for Youth Engagement

Dos	Don'ts
Create informative and engaging content that fits the platform.	Try too hard to use slang or force memes.
Use real officers and community leaders in videos to build trust.	Overuse trending challenges without context.
Engage in interactive content, such as polls and Q&As.	Ignore or delete critical comments without addressing concerns.
Utilize short-form videos (TikTok, Instagram Reels) to educate on relevant topics.	Rely solely on press-style statements without personalization.
Collaborate with youth influencers or student groups for credibility.	Post content that feels overly scripted or inauthentic.

How Agencies Can Communicate Effectively on Gen Z-Dominated Platforms

1. Understanding Platform Preferences

- **TikTok & Instagram Reels** – Best for short-form video content, storytelling, humor, and quick tips. Example: A law enforcement agency could create a **"Day in the Life of a Police Officer"** video series showing different aspects of an officer's daily responsibilities in a fun, relatable way.
- **YouTube Shorts** – Ideal for in-depth educational content. Example: Posting short videos explaining **what to do when pulled over by an officer**, how to **stay safe at public events**, or breaking down **common legal misconceptions**.
- **Snapchat** – Useful for real-time updates and informal engagement. Example: Using Snapchat Stories to highlight **officer participation in community events** or to share **crime prevention tips** in an engaging, behind-the-scenes format.
- **Discord & Reddit** – Great for engaging in non-authoritative, informal discussions. Example: Agencies could participate in **AMA (Ask Me Anything) sessions** on Reddit, allowing users to ask law enforcement officers questions in an open and transparent format.

2. Prioritizing Storytelling Over Traditional Announcements

- Instead of generic crime prevention posts, use **real-world scenarios** to educate young users. Example: A TikTok video series featuring officers **debunking crime myths**, such as "Can I get arrested for filming the police?" or "What should I do if I lose my ID at a concert?"
- Feature **officer-led content** that shows a behind-the-scenes look at policing. Example: Showcasing a **K9 unit in action**, a **training simulation**, or a **ride-along experience** in a casual, vlog-style format.

- Create **"day in the life" videos** to humanize officers and their roles. Example: A school resource officer could film **a walk-through of their day**, interacting with students and discussing their role in campus safety.

---

3. Leveraging Humor & Relatable Content

- Light-hearted content can be effective but must align with the agency's professional standards. Example: A police department could participate in a **safe driving challenge on TikTok** featuring officers performing skits about distracted driving.
- Self-awareness is key—acknowledge cultural trends without trying too hard. Example: Instead of awkwardly dancing to a viral TikTok trend, an officer could do a **reaction video explaining the importance of situational awareness**.
- Avoid forced memes or outdated internet slang that may come across as disingenuous. Example: Instead of forcing a joke, an agency could **create a relatable story-based post about internet safety** that speaks naturally to young audiences.

---

4. Encouraging Interaction & Participation

- Conduct live Q&A sessions where younger audiences can ask officers direct questions. Example: Hosting an **Instagram Live or TikTok Q&A session** where officers answer questions about laws, policing, or career paths in law enforcement.
- Use **polls, challenges, and interactive content** to engage users. Example: Posting a **scenario-based Instagram poll** like "What would you do if you saw someone shoplifting?" followed by an explainer post on how to report crimes responsibly.
- Respond to comments and create discussions rather than just posting information. Example: If a young person asks about curfew laws in their city, **replying with accurate, easy-to-understand information** and directing them to resources.

5. Collaborating with Influencers & Community Figures

- Partner with local influencers who resonate with younger audiences. Example: Working with **popular TikTok creators or student athletes** to share safety messages in a way that feels natural and trustworthy.
- Engage with student leaders, youth groups, and school programs for broader outreach. Example: Hosting **a collaborative event with a school's student government** to educate students on safety and personal rights.
- Feature young voices in public safety messaging to improve relatability. Example: Inviting **teen volunteers or youth police cadets** to share their perspectives on community safety via social media takeovers.

Mistakes to Avoid When Trying to Be "Relatable"

1. Trying Too Hard to Be Trendy

- Overusing slang or outdated memes can backfire and make agencies seem out of touch.
- Instead of forcing humor, focus on content that **naturally resonates** with younger audiences.

2. Ignoring Serious Topics

- While humor can be engaging, some issues require a serious, respectful tone.
- Balance engaging content with educational and awareness-driven messaging.

3. Overproducing Content

- Younger audiences prefer **authentic, raw content** over highly polished, corporate-style videos.
- Officers speaking directly to the camera in a conversational manner are often more effective than scripted content.

4. Failing to Listen and Adapt

- Engagement is a two-way street—listen to feedback and evolve content accordingly.
- Monitor social media conversations to understand emerging trends and concerns.

Best Practices for Law Enforcement Engagement with Younger Audiences

- **Be Consistent and Authentic** – Engage regularly and genuinely without appearing as if you're just following trends.

- **Incorporate Real Voices** – Feature actual officers, community leaders, and youth in your content rather than relying solely on institutional messaging.

- **Showcase Relatable Scenarios** – Present situations that younger audiences encounter, such as traffic stops, online safety, and reporting suspicious activity.

- **Use Engaging Visuals and Multimedia** – High-quality photos, infographics, and well-produced videos help make content more compelling.

- **Educate Through Entertainment** – Gamify safety tips, use interactive quizzes, or present serious topics in an engaging manner that resonates with younger audiences.

The Road Ahead

Engaging younger audiences is about meeting them where they are, understanding their digital culture, and fostering trust through authenticity. Agencies that successfully adapt will not only increase engagement but also build stronger community relationships for the future.

Law Enforcement as a Community Resource

The Shift from Reactive to Proactive Social Media Engagement

Many law enforcement agencies primarily use social media for crime updates, emergency alerts, and press releases. While these are essential, agencies can increase community trust and engagement by also using their platforms as **a public safety resource**. This means shifting from a **reactive** approach—where social media is only used when something happens—to a **proactive** strategy that educates, informs, and empowers the community daily.

Why Law Enforcement Should Focus on Being a Community Resource:

- **Builds Public Trust** – Regular, non-crime-related content fosters goodwill and reduces negative perceptions of law enforcement.
- **Reduces Misinformation** – Providing clear, accurate explanations of laws and procedures can prevent community confusion.
- **Encourages Civic Participation** – Educating the public on their rights, local ordinances, and safety measures strengthens community involvement.
- **Enhances Crime Prevention Efforts** – Teaching people how to avoid becoming victims of crime is just as important as responding to crimes.
- **Reinforces Community Partnerships** – Showcasing collaborations with local organizations, schools, and businesses highlights the agency's commitment to public service.

How to Pivot Social Media Content Toward Education and Public Resources

1. Explainers on How Investigations Work

- **Example:** A video series called **"Behind the Badge"**, explaining common law enforcement procedures, such as:
  - What happens when someone reports a crime?
  - How do officers determine if an arrest should be made?
  - What's the process for handling evidence?
- **Example:** A Facebook Live Q&A with detectives explaining how they solve cases, followed by community-submitted questions.

2. Public Safety Workshops & Virtual Events

- **Example:** Hosting monthly safety webinars on topics like **self-defense**, **cybersecurity**, or **home security tips**.
- **Example:** A TikTok challenge where community members share their own safety tips, with officers reacting or adding expert insights.
- **Example:** Partnering with local schools for a **"Teen Traffic Safety Week"**, featuring daily Instagram Reels covering topics like impaired driving, seat belt importance, and how to handle a traffic stop.

3. Debunking Legal Myths & Addressing Misinformation

- **Example:** A social media campaign called **"Fact vs. Fiction: Law Enforcement Edition"**, where officers break down common misconceptions like:
  - "You must answer all police questions." (Not true, you have the right to remain silent.)
  - "Police need a warrant for any search." (Not always—officers can search under certain exceptions.)

- **Example:** A TikTok series featuring an officer reacting to viral misinformation videos and explaining the real laws behind them.

---

4. Crime Prevention Tips & Awareness Campaigns

- **Example:** A series of Instagram carousels called **"Protect Yourself"**, featuring:
  - How to recognize online scams and phishing attempts.
  - Ways to prevent package theft during the holidays.
  - How to spot and report suspicious activity.
- **Example:** A Facebook community group where officers provide **weekly crime trends and prevention tips**, allowing residents to ask questions and share concerns.

---

5. Highlighting Available Community Resources

- **Example:** Regularly posting about **mental health hotlines, victim advocacy programs, addiction recovery services, and domestic violence resources**.
- **Example:** A YouTube series called **"Know Your City"**, where officers showcase local support services, explaining:
  - Where to get free legal aid.
  - How to access food assistance programs.
  - What to do if someone needs emergency shelter.

---

6. Youth & Family Engagement Content

- **Example:** A weekly segment called **"Ask a Cop"**, where kids send in questions, and officers answer them in short, engaging TikTok videos.
- **Example:** A Snapchat series featuring **school resource officers discussing school safety, bullying prevention, and student rights**.

- **Example:** A community contest where children **draw safety posters**, with the winning designs featured on the department's social media and website.

The Road Ahead

Law enforcement agencies must evolve from being just **a news source for crime reports** to becoming **a trusted community resource**. By prioritizing educational content, public safety messaging, and engagement-based initiatives, agencies can build **stronger relationships, increase trust, and enhance public safety in meaningful ways**.

In the next chapter, we will explore **case studies of successful law enforcement social media strategies**, breaking down what works, what doesn't, and how agencies can adapt best practices to fit their own communities.

Appendix A:
Case Studies and Agencies to Watch

Learning from Real-World Successes

Social media strategies evolve, but the principles of engagement, transparency, and crisis communication remain constant. These updated case studies highlight how law enforcement agencies have successfully navigated social media in recent years and what lessons can be applied moving forward.

Case Study: Rye Police Department

The Power of TikTok for Community Engagement

How Rye PD Used TikTok to Connect with the Public

In 2024, Rye Police Department emerged as one of the most followed law enforcement agencies on TikTok, amassing over **500K followers** by leveraging short-form video content. Unlike traditional social media posts that focus solely on official announcements, Rye PD took a different approach: showcasing the human side of policing.

Their Strategy:

- **Humor & Relatability** – Officers participated in TikTok challenges, but with a policing twist, such as integrating **crime prevention tips into trending dance videos**.
- **Behind-the-Scenes Footage** – Weekly vlogs provided an inside look at community policing efforts.
- **Engagement-Focused Content** – Officers actively responded to comments, participated in duets, and answered user-submitted questions.

The Impact:

- **60% increase in youth engagement** with local teens actively interacting with the department.
- **Widespread media recognition**, with major outlets covering their viral campaigns.
- **Expanded reach beyond their jurisdiction**, leading to increased trust and community support.

Key Takeaways:

- **Relatability builds engagement** – Show the human side of law enforcement.
- **Short-form video is king** – TikTok, Instagram Reels, and YouTube Shorts outperform static content.
- **Participate in trends, but stay professional** – Not every viral trend is appropriate for law enforcement.

Case Study: Miami-Dade PD

Social Media as a Public Safety Tool

How Miami-Dade PD Mastered Crisis Communication Online

In 2023, Miami-Dade PD set the standard for using social media during public safety crises, particularly during hurricane season. Their strategic use of **Facebook Live, YouTube Live, and Twitter Spaces** allowed them to provide real-time updates, debunk misinformation, and keep the public informed throughout severe weather events.

Their Strategy:

- **Live Q&A Sessions** – Instead of just posting weather warnings, officers engaged directly with the public through live town hall Q&As.
- **Partnerships with Local Media & Influencers** – Collaborated with news outlets and community figures to amplify messages.
- **Misinformation Control** – Proactively monitored discussions and corrected false information before it spread widely.

The Impact:

- **Public trust increased**, as people saw law enforcement providing direct, real-time responses.
- **A 50% reduction in misinformation spread** during emergencies.
- **Over 1 million views** on hurricane preparedness livestreams.

Key Takeaways:

- **Social media is a critical emergency response tool** – Agencies must prepare a crisis communication plan in advance.
- **Live-streaming increases credibility** – Facebook Live and YouTube Live allow for real-time, direct interaction.
- **Collaboration expands reach** – Partnering with local media and influencers extends the impact of public safety messaging.

Case Study: Seattle PD

Mastering Crisis Communication on Social Media

How Seattle PD Became the Gold Standard for Misinformation Management

During a major public safety incident in 2023, Seattle PD successfully controlled misinformation using social media. The department quickly addressed **a rapidly spreading online rumor about an officer-involved incident**, preventing false narratives from dominating the conversation.

Their Strategy:

- **First-Response Posting** – Seattle PD **posted official information first**, ensuring their narrative was established before speculation spread.
- **Pinned Posts & Story Highlights** – Kept critical updates at the top of their Twitter/X feed and Instagram Stories for easy access.
- **Proactive Media Coordination** – Worked closely with journalists and community leaders to ensure accurate information was amplified.

The Impact:

- **Misinformation was quickly debunked**, preventing widespread confusion.
- **Community trust increased**, as Seattle PD showed a commitment to transparency.
- **Law enforcement agencies nationwide** began using their strategy as a model for crisis communication.

Key Takeaways:

- **Agencies must post first to control the narrative** – If law enforcement doesn't, misinformation will fill the gap.
- **Crisis updates need multi-platform coverage** – Information should be available on Twitter, Facebook, Instagram, and official websites.
- **Pinned posts and Story Highlights improve visibility** – Keeping key updates accessible reduces confusion.

Case Study: Portland Police Bureau
PPB Central Bike Squad – A Model for Engaging & Professional Social Media Presence

How PPB Central Bike Squad Built a Successful Social Media Presence

The Portland Police Bureau (PPB) Central Bike Squad has created an **engaging, community-focused social media strategy** that balances **professionalism and humor**. Unlike traditional law enforcement accounts, they **humanize officers, showcase positive interactions, and foster direct community engagement**.

Their Strategy:

- **Dedicated Social Media Officer** – One officer rides with the squad, capturing real-time footage and crafting engaging posts.
- **Mix of Humor & Professionalism** – Posts include **witty captions and lighthearted content**, alongside safety messages.
- **Community Engagement** – Highlights partnerships with local businesses, features user-submitted stories, and recognizes acts of goodwill.

The Impact:

- **Grew a highly loyal following**, with consistently high engagement rates.
- **Respected by both the public and elected officials**, leading to greater community support.
- **Inspired other agencies** to adopt similar storytelling approaches.

Key Takeaways:

- **Transparency and authenticity matter** – People engage more with genuine, behind-the-scenes content.
- **Humor can build trust** – Lighthearted posts, when appropriate, humanize officers.
- **A dedicated social media officer improves engagement** – Consistency is key.

Agencies to Watch

Several police agencies have distinguished themselves as leaders in social media engagement. Their strategies can serve as models for law enforcement agencies looking to improve their digital outreach.

Agency	Platform & Follower Count	Key Social Media Strengths
New York Police Department (NYPD)	Instagram: 624K+ followers	Behind-the-scenes content, community engagement, real-time updates.
Los Angeles Police Department (LAPD)	Twitter: 1M+ followers	Misinformation control, media relations, breaking news updates.
San Antonio Police Department (SAPD)	Facebook: 200K+ followers	Humor-driven engagement, interactive posts, community partnerships.
Pasco County Sheriff's Office	Twitter: 300K+ followers	Real-time engagement, humorous yet professional tone, strong public trust.
Philadelphia Police Department	Twitter: 200K+ followers	Public safety campaigns, missing persons alerts, high community interaction.

Key Lessons from Top Agencies:

- **Timely Information Dissemination** – Keeping the public informed with real-time updates builds trust.
- **Community Engagement** – Interactive, relatable content fosters strong community relationships.
- **Transparency & Professionalism** – Openly sharing departmental operations enhances credibility.

Final Thoughts

By analyzing successful case studies and top-performing agencies, law enforcement departments can refine their social media strategies to **increase trust, boost engagement, and enhance public safety communication**. The key is to remain **consistent, transparent, and adaptable** to evolving digital landscapes.

Appendix B:
Social Media Worksheets

Introduction

The following worksheets are designed to help law enforcement agencies **strategically plan, execute, and evaluate** their social media efforts in 2025. These tools provide a structured approach to content creation, audience engagement, security best practices, and crisis communication preparedness.

With the rapid evolution of digital platforms, maintaining an **effective and professional social media presence** requires consistency, adaptability, and clear objectives. These worksheets will guide agencies in:

- Developing **weekly content plans** to maintain an active and engaging presence.

- Evaluating the effectiveness of each **social media platform** and making data-driven improvements.

- Conducting **social media audits** to ensure alignment with department goals and public engagement needs.

- Preparing for **crisis situations**, ensuring that accurate information is shared efficiently.

By using these worksheets as a foundational framework, agencies can **enhance public trust, optimize their outreach strategies, and navigate the digital landscape with confidence.**

To print out copies of these worksheets visit:
LESMCoach.com/Worksheets

Weekly Content Planning Worksheet

Use this worksheet to plan your agency's social media content for the week. Incorporate **emergency updates** as needed. The same content can go on multiple platforms, but you may need to adjust it to work.

Idea	Medium	Platform	Day	Goal
Officer Safety Tip	Short Video	Instagram	M	Education
Crime Trend Infographic	Image	Nextdoor	T	Awareness

EXAMPLES

Social Media Channel Planner

Use this to **evaluate and improve** your agency's presence on different social media platforms.

Today's Date: _____   Review Date: _____

(6 months from today.)

Platform:_____

_____

Primary Platform Demographics:

      Age: _____

      Gender: _____

      Geography: _____

_____

Goals for this Platform:

_____

Strategies for this Platform:

Social Media Strategic Plan

1. Who is on the social media team?

List key personnel responsible for content creation, engagement, and crisis communication.

2. What are your social media keywords?

Identify terms that should be **monitored** and **tracked** to understand community sentiment.

3. What are your goals?

Define **SMART goals** for social media outreach, engagement, and crisis response.

4. How will you measure success?

- Engagement rate

- Response time to public inquiries

- Accuracy in crisis communication

- Growth of audience and trust levels

5. Who is your primary audience?

Understand **who your agency is serving on each platform** and tailor content accordingly.

6. What makes your agency's social media presence unique?

Define what **sets your department apart** in digital engagement.

7. How will you humanize your agency?

Incorporate **real stories, officer highlights, and interactive content** into your strategy.

8. What is your crisis communication plan?

Develop **pre-drafted emergency messages** for disasters, active threats, and misinformation control.

Agency Social Media Audit Worksheet

General Information

- **Date of Audit:** _____

- **Next Review Date:** *(6 months from today)* _____

- **Platform Being Reviewed:** _____

Performance Metrics

- **Follower Growth:** _____

- **Top-Performing Posts:** _____

- **Engagement Rates:** _____

- **Average Response Time to Comments/Inquiries:** _____

Opportunities for Improvement

- **New platform considerations:** (e.g., Should we start engaging on Threads?)

- **Better content mix?** (e.g., Do we need more short-form video?)

- **Enhanced security measures?** (e.g., Stronger admin control over accounts?)

Agency Self-Assessment:
Digital Readiness for Law Enforcement

Purpose

This self-assessment tool helps law enforcement agencies determine their current level of readiness in key areas of digital communication, public engagement, and misinformation management. By evaluating these areas, agencies can identify strengths and areas for improvement, leading to more effective and trusted online interactions with the community.

Instructions

Rate your agency's preparedness in each category on a scale of **1 to 5**, where:

1 = Needs significant improvement
2 = Developing, but inconsistent
3 = Moderate readiness, room for improvement
4 = Strong implementation, minor refinements needed
5 = Fully optimized and effective

Assessment Categories

1. Misinformation Management

- We have a protocol for identifying and correcting misinformation online.
- Our team actively monitors social media for false narratives.
- We have designated personnel responsible for issuing corrections and clarifications.
- We collaborate with trusted media sources to counter misinformation.
- We use infographics, videos, or other engaging formats to clarify key issues.

Score: ___/5

2. Crisis Communication Readiness

- We have pre-drafted emergency response templates for social media.
- Our agency can provide real-time updates during a crisis.
- Leadership is trained in effective public communication during high-stress events.
- We use a multi-platform approach (Twitter, Facebook, Nextdoor, etc.) to disseminate information.
- We evaluate our crisis response efforts after each major incident and make improvements.

Score: ___/5

3. Public Engagement & Community Interaction

- Our agency regularly responds to public inquiries on social media.
- We hold live Q&A sessions, town halls, or engagement events to build trust.
- We use storytelling techniques to humanize law enforcement efforts.
- Officers participate in community-driven initiatives and share experiences online.
- We have a structured approach to handling online criticism and negative comments.

Score: ___/5

4. Digital Security & Cyber Threat Preparedness

- Multi-factor authentication (MFA) is enabled on all social media accounts.
- Our staff is trained in identifying phishing attempts and social engineering attacks.
- We conduct regular cybersecurity audits of our digital communication channels.
- Our agency has a recovery plan in case of account compromise or hacking.
- We monitor for fake or impersonation accounts and report them promptly.

Score: ___/5

5. Content Strategy & Messaging Consistency

- We follow a content calendar for regular updates and announcements.
- Posts align with our agency's core values and strategic goals.
- We tailor content to different platforms and audience demographics.
- We analyze engagement metrics and refine our approach accordingly.
- Our agency avoids forced trends and focuses on authentic messaging.

Score: ___/5

Scoring & Next Steps

Total Score: Add up the scores across all categories.

Interpretation:

- **5-10**: High priority for improvement—consider formal training and strategy revisions.
- **11-20**: Moderate readiness—some gaps exist, refine policies and engagement tactics.
- **21-25**: Strong performance—continue refining and expanding best practices.

By assessing these areas, agencies can create targeted action plans to enhance their digital trust, engagement, and crisis communication capabilities.

Crisis Response Templates for Law Enforcement

Purpose: These templates provide pre-written social media messages for law enforcement agencies to ensure timely, clear, and accurate communication during emergencies.

---

1. Active Threat / Violent Incidents

Initial Alert:

" EMERGENCY ALERT: Officers are responding to an active incident at [location]. Please **avoid the area** and follow this page for official updates."

Follow-Up (If Shelter-in-Place Required):

"**SHELTER-IN-PLACE ORDER:** Residents near [location] should **stay indoors, lock doors, and remain away from windows**. Updates will follow from law enforcement officials."

Resolution Statement:

"The situation at [location] has been resolved. Officers will remain in the area for investigation. Thank you for your patience and cooperation."

---

2. Misinformation Correction

"We are aware of misinformation circulating about [incident]. The verified facts are as follows: [brief factual summary]. Please rely on official law enforcement sources for accurate updates. If you have questions, please contact [agency contact]."

3. Severe Weather & Natural Disasters

Pre-Event Warning:

" ⚠️ **SEVERE WEATHER ALERT:** Hazardous conditions are expected in [area] due to [event: flood, hurricane, wildfire, etc.]. Stay informed and prepare accordingly. Key safety tips: [link to resources]. Updates will follow as conditions change."

During Event:

"[Weather event] has caused hazardous conditions in [location]. **Avoid travel unless absolutely necessary.** Emergency crews are working to restore safety. Updates will be posted as the situation evolves."

Post-Event / Recovery Message:

"[Weather event] has passed, but hazards remain. Avoid [specific roads/ areas] due to [flooding, debris, power lines, etc.]. If you need assistance, contact [emergency resource]."

4. Missing Person / Endangered Individual Alert

" 🚨 **MISSING PERSON ALERT:** [Name], age [X], was last seen at [location] on [date/time]. Description: [height, weight, clothing, distinguishing features]. If seen, call [agency contact] immediately. Please share to help locate them safely."

5. Public Safety Incidents (Road Closures, Hazards, Evacuations)

Road Closure Notice:

"🚧 **ROAD CLOSED:** Due to [incident: accident, flooding, downed power lines], [road name] is closed between [start location] and [end location]. Use alternate routes and expect delays."

Hazard Warning:

" ⚠ A [hazard: chemical spill, downed power lines, fire] has been reported at [location]. Officers and emergency personnel are on scene. Please **stay clear** until further notice for your safety."

Evacuation Order:

" 🚪 **MANDATORY EVACUATION:** Due to [fire/flood/etc.], residents in [specific area] should evacuate immediately to [designated shelter location]. Follow law enforcement instructions for safe evacuation."

6. Traffic and DUI Enforcement Alerts

"🚗 **DUI ENFORCEMENT TONIGHT:** Officers will be conducting increased DUI patrols in [area] from [start time] to [end time]. Make the right choice—designate a driver or use a rideshare. #DriveSober #StaySafe"

"🚧 **TRAFFIC #ALERT:** Expect increased enforcement in [area] targeting [speeding/distracted driving/school zone violations] today. Drive safely and follow posted limits."

7. Cybercrime / Scam Warnings

"⚠ **SCAM ALERT:** Be aware of [current scam, e.g., fake police donations, IRS fraud calls]. Official agencies will NEVER [request payments via gift cards, threaten arrest, etc.]. If contacted, do not provide personal information and report suspicious activity to [agency contact]."

8. Scam / Fraud Warnings

Phone Scam Alert:

"📵 **SCAM ALERT:** We are hearing reports of a scam where callers **pretend to be 'Officer Smith'** from [Department Name], asking for money or personal information. **This is fake.** Law enforcement will never call demanding payments. If you receive this call, **hang up and report it** to [agency contact]."

Online Scam Warning:

"⚠ **FRAUD ALERT:** Scammers are posing as [agency name] online, sending fake donation requests or fines. **We will never ask for payments via gift cards, Venmo, or wire transfers.** If you receive a suspicious message, do not engage—report it to [contact info]."

9. Fire / Wildfire Response & Road Closures

Wildfire Risk Alert:

"🔥 **FIRE WEATHER WARNING:** Conditions are favorable for wildfires in [area]. Avoid outdoor burning, dispose of cigarettes properly, and report any suspicious smoke to [fire agency contact]. For real-time updates, follow @FireAgency."

Active Wildfire Response:

"📵 **WILDFIRE ALERT:** Fire crews are responding to an active wildfire at [location]. **Evacuations may be necessary.** Avoid the area and follow

@FireAgency for emergency updates. We will share critical public safety information as it becomes available."

Road Closure Notice (Fire-Related):

"🚧 **ROAD CLOSURE:** Due to fire activity, [road name] is closed between [point A] and [point B]. Firefighters and officers are on scene. **Use alternate routes** and check @FireAgency for further updates."

10. Traffic & DUI Enforcement Alerts

Seat Belt Enforcement:

"🚗 **SAFETY BELT MISSION:** Officers will be conducting a **seat belt enforcement operation** in [location] today. **Buckle up—every trip, every time.** It's the law, and it saves lives. #ClickItOrTicket"

School Zone Enforcement:

"🚸 **SLOW DOWN!** Officers are monitoring school zones in [area] to ensure drivers obey speed limits and stop for crossing guards. **Let's keep our kids safe.** #DriveSafe #SchoolZoneSafety"

DUI Enforcement Notice:

"🚓 **DUI PATROLS TONIGHT:** Extra officers will be out in [area] looking for impaired drivers. **Make the right choice—don't drink and drive.** Use a designated driver or rideshare. #DriveSober #DUIEnforcement"

Traffic Safety Reminder:

"⚠ **REMINDER:** Speeding, distracted driving, and DUI contribute to [X]% of crashes in [area]. **Slow down, focus on the road, and make it home safely.** #ZeroFatalities #DriveSmart"

11. Crime & Community Alerts

Suspicious Activity Alert:

"👀 **BE ON ALERT:** Officers are investigating reports of suspicious activity in [area]. If you see anything unusual, call [non-emergency number] or 911 for emergencies. **Community awareness keeps us all safe.**"

Theft Prevention Reminder:

"🚗 **LOCK IT OR LOSE IT:** Car break-ins are preventable! Remove valuables, lock doors, and park in well-lit areas. Thieves target easy opportunities—don't give them one. #CrimePrevention"

Holiday Shopping Safety:

"🎁 **HOLIDAY SAFETY TIP:** Thieves are watching for easy targets! Keep purchases out of sight, don't leave your car running unattended, and be aware of your surroundings. Report suspicious activity to [non-emergency number]. #StaySafe"

12. Emergency & Evacuation Notices

Hazardous Spill / Shelter-in-Place:

"⚠️ **HAZMAT INCIDENT:** A hazardous materials spill has been reported at [location]. **Shelter in place, close all windows, and avoid the area.** Emergency crews are responding. Updates will follow."

Evacuation Notice:

"🚨 **MANDATORY EVACUATION:** Due to [fire, flood, etc.], residents in [specific area] must evacuate immediately. Go to [designated shelter] and follow emergency personnel instructions. For updates, follow @EmergencyAgency."

13. Weather-Related Public Safety Messages

Extreme Heat Advisory:

" ☀ **HEAT WARNING:** Temperatures in [area] will exceed [X]°F today. Stay hydrated, limit outdoor activities, and check on vulnerable neighbors. Cooling centers are available at [locations]. For updates, follow @WeatherAgency."

Flooding & Road Safety:

" 🌧 **FLOOD WARNING:** Heavy rain has caused flooding in [specific area]. **Do not drive through floodwaters!** Turn around, don't drown. For road conditions, follow @TrafficAgency."

Winter Storm Travel Advisory:

" ❄ **WINTER WEATHER ALERT:** Roads in [area] are icy and dangerous. Avoid travel if possible. **If you must drive, reduce speed, increase distance, and carry emergency supplies.** For road closures, follow @DOT."

14. Major Event / Large Crowd Safety

Public Event Safety Tips:

" 🎆 **HEADED TO [EVENT NAME]?** Expect large crowds and increased police presence. **Stay aware of your surroundings, keep belongings secure, and report anything suspicious to officers on-site.** Enjoy safely! #EventSafety"

Lost Child / Reunification Area:

" 👮 **LOST CHILD REUNIFICATION:** If you're at [event] and get separated from your child, **head to [designated area] where officers will assist.** Teach your kids to identify police or security staff for help."

15. Public Messaging & Encouragement

Back-to-School Safety Message:

"🎒 **BACK TO SCHOOL REMINDER:** Drivers, **watch for children and school buses.** Parents, remind kids about pedestrian safety. **Officers will be in school zones to help keep everyone safe!** #BackToSchoolSafety"

Thanking the Public After an Incident:

"🙏 **THANK YOU, COMMUNITY!** Your cooperation helped officers resolve [incident] quickly. We appreciate your vigilance and commitment to safety. Stay informed and stay safe!"

16. Dignitary Visits & High-Profile Events

Initial Public Awareness:

"🚗 **DIGNITARY VISIT ALERT:** A high-profile visitor will be in [area] on [date]. Expect increased security, road closures, and temporary traffic delays. We appreciate your cooperation in ensuring a safe event. Follow this page for real-time updates. #PublicSafety"

Security Reminder:

"⚠️ **DIGNITARY VISIT - SECURITY NOTICE:** Officers will be working closely with federal and state partners to ensure safety during [event]. Expect security screenings, restricted access areas, and a visible law enforcement presence. **If you see something suspicious, say something.** Call [non-emergency number] or 911 in an emergency."

Traffic Impact & Road Closures:

"🚧 **TRAFFIC ADVISORY:** Due to the visit of [dignitary], roads in [specific areas] will be closed from [start time] to [end time]. Expect significant delays, especially around [location]. Use alternate routes and plan ahead. For real-time traffic updates, follow @TrafficAgency."

Public Viewing Areas / Event Logistics:

"🎤 **ATTENDING THE EVENT?** Public viewing areas for [dignitary's visit] will be at [location]. Arrive early, expect security screenings, and follow all directions from officers. No large bags or prohibited items allowed. For full event details, visit [link]."

Protest & Demonstration Guidance (If Applicable):

"📣 **PLANNING TO PROTEST?** We respect the right to peaceful assembly. Officers will be present to ensure safety for all. Please remain lawful, avoid blocking roadways, and follow all instructions from law enforcement."

Thank You / Recap After Event:

"✅ **DIGNITARY VISIT CONCLUDED:** The visit of [dignitary] to [area] has safely concluded. Thank you to our community for your patience during road closures and security measures. Officers remain in the area as normal operations resume."

Sample Social Media Policy

Purpose

This policy establishes guidelines for the **responsible, ethical, and secure** use of social media by [Agency Name] to promote transparency, community engagement, and public safety while safeguarding sensitive information and maintaining professionalism.

Scope

This policy applies to **all employees, sworn and civilian**, who manage or contribute to official agency social media accounts, as well as those who engage with the public on digital platforms in an official capacity.

Official Agency Accounts

1. Account Management

- All official social media accounts must be **approved** and **monitored** by the designated Public Information Officer (PIO) or Social Media Team.
- **Administrative access** will be granted only to **authorized personnel**, with login credentials securely stored and updated every 90 days.
- Agency accounts must clearly **identify themselves** as official law enforcement pages, with appropriate logos and disclaimers.
-

2. Content Guidelines

All content posted on agency accounts must:

- Be **factual, timely, and relevant** to public safety and community engagement.

- Adhere to **department policies, state laws, and federal regulations**.

- Maintain **professionalism** and avoid language that is inflammatory, biased, or inappropriate.

- Protect **confidential and legally restricted information** (e.g., ongoing investigations, victim identities, personnel records).

- Credit and verify **external sources** before sharing third-party content.

3. Acceptable Uses of Social Media

Approved uses of agency social media accounts include:

- **Public Safety Announcements** (crime prevention tips, weather alerts, missing persons, road closures).
- **Community Engagement** (events, officer spotlights, department initiatives).
- **Emergency Notifications** (active threats, evacuations, crisis updates).
- **Recruitment Efforts** (hiring campaigns, career opportunities).
- **Myth-Busting & Misinformation Correction** (countering false narratives with verified facts).

Employee Personal Use & Conduct

4. Guidelines for Personal Accounts

Employees are **encouraged to exercise caution** when engaging on social media in a personal capacity. While off-duty employees have **First Amendment rights**, the following guidelines apply:

- **Do not** disclose confidential agency information.

- **Avoid conduct that undermines public trust** in law enforcement (e.g., hate speech, harassment, political endorsements that imply agency affiliation).
- **Clearly state that opinions are personal** and do not represent [Agency Name] when discussing law enforcement topics.
- **Do not engage in online disputes** or debates that could reflect negatively on the agency.

Crisis & Emergency Communication

5. Crisis Social Media Protocols

During major incidents, agency social media will serve as an **official communication channel**. To ensure accuracy and consistency:

- Only **designated personnel** may post during a crisis.
- Use **pre-approved templates** for emergency alerts.
- **Pin important updates** to the top of agency pages.
- Correct **misinformation swiftly** using official sources.
- Coordinate with **local news and partner agencies** to amplify messages.

Security & Compliance

6. Cybersecurity & Account Protection

To prevent unauthorized access and account breaches:

- Enable **multi-factor authentication (MFA)** on all accounts.
- Update **passwords every 90 days** and prohibit sharing login credentials.
- Regularly audit **access permissions** and remove former employees.
- Monitor for **fake or impersonation accounts** and report them immediately.

7. Compliance with Public Records Laws

- All social media activity is **subject to public records laws** and must be archived for compliance.
- Deleting public comments must follow **First Amendment considerations** and agency moderation policies.
- Private messages or direct inquiries related to investigations must be **logged and documented** accordingly.

Violations & Enforcement

8. Disciplinary Actions

Violations of this policy may result in:

- **Warnings, retraining, or suspension** of social media privileges.
- **Formal disciplinary action** for breaches involving confidential information, unprofessional conduct, or misuse of agency resources.
- **Legal consequences** for violations of state or federal laws regarding information security or discrimination.

Review & Updates

This policy will be **reviewed annually** by the Social Media Team and agency leadership to ensure compliance with **current laws, platform changes, and best practices**.

Acknowledgment

I, **[Employee Name]**, acknowledge that I have read and understand the **[Agency Name] Social Media Policy** and agree to comply with its provisions.

Signature: _____

Date: _____

Appendix D:
Emerging Platforms

Introduction

New social media platforms continue to emerge, offering unique ways for law enforcement to engage with the public. While established platforms like Facebook, Twitter/X, and TikTok remain critical, these newer platforms provide opportunities to reach different demographics and adapt to shifting online behaviors.

1. Threads

- **What It Is:** Meta's alternative to Twitter/X, focused on text-based conversations.
- **Key Features:** No ads yet, integrated with Instagram, and designed for public discourse.
- **How Law Enforcement Can Use It:** Engage in real-time discussions, provide updates on incidents, and combat misinformation.

2. Bluesky

- **What It Is:** A decentralized social media platform similar to Twitter/X, backed by Twitter's co-founder.
- **Key Features:** Open-source, customizable content moderation, and algorithmic flexibility.
- **How Law Enforcement Can Use It:** Share official information in a less restrictive, more user-controlled environment.

3. Mastodon

- **What It Is:** A decentralized, non-algorithmic social media platform where users join different "instances."

- **Key Features:** No central authority, user-controlled content moderation, and open-source infrastructure.
- **How Law Enforcement Can Use It:** Post updates in community-driven instances and interact in specialized public safety groups.

4. YouTube Shorts

- **What It Is:** YouTube's answer to TikTok and Instagram Reels, offering short-form video content.
- **Key Features:** Short videos (up to 60 seconds), vertical format, high engagement potential.
- **How Law Enforcement Can Use It:** Share quick safety tips, crime prevention videos, and behind-the-scenes department content.

5. Instagram Stories

- **What It Is:** Temporary 24-hour posts that allow for real-time updates and interactive engagement.
- **Key Features:** Polls, Q&As, location tagging, and disappearing content after 24 hours.
- **How Law Enforcement Can Use It:** Use Stories for urgent updates, quick polls, and behind-the-scenes insights into department operations.

6. Instagram Reels

- **What It Is:** A feature for short, engaging vertical videos similar to TikTok.
- **Key Features:** Algorithm-driven reach, editing tools, music overlays, and up to 90-second videos.
- **How Law Enforcement Can Use It:** Post crime prevention tips, officer spotlights, and recruitment videos to increase engagement.

7. Discord

- **What It Is:** A chat-based platform originally for gamers but now widely used for community discussions.
- **Key Features:** Private and public servers, voice/video chat, and highly engaged communities.

- **How Law Enforcement Can Use It:** Build community engagement hubs for crime prevention discussions or emergency preparedness groups.

8. Nextdoor

- **What It Is:** A hyperlocal social platform for neighborhood-based discussions.
- **Key Features:** Verified community members, location-based groups, and law enforcement-specific pages.
- **How Law Enforcement Can Use It:** Post localized alerts, safety updates, and community outreach messages.

9. BeReal

- **What It Is:** A social media app promoting unfiltered, real-life moments by requiring users to post spontaneous photos daily.
- **Key Features:** Authentic content, no filters, and no permanent feeds.
- **How Law Enforcement Can Use It:** Humanize officers by sharing candid, behind-the-scenes looks at daily operations.

10. Snapchat

- **What It Is:** A multimedia messaging app known for disappearing messages and Stories.
- **Key Features:** Ephemeral content, location-based features, and private messaging.
- **How Law Enforcement Can Use It:** Share real-time updates, community alerts, and engage younger audiences with safety messages.

11. Reddit

- **What It Is:** A forum-based platform with thousands of niche communities (subreddits).
- **Key Features:** Upvoting/downvoting system, long-form discussions, and AMA (Ask Me Anything) sessions.

- **How Law Enforcement Can Use It:** Host AMAs for transparency, answer legal and safety-related questions, and monitor community concerns.

12. Twitch

- **What It Is:** A live-streaming platform primarily focused on gaming but expanding to broader content.
- **Key Features:** Live interaction with audiences, chat functions, and community-building tools.
- **How Law Enforcement Can Use It:** Stream public safety Q&As, engage younger audiences, and provide educational programming.

TikTok Restrictions and Alternatives

- **Why Some Agencies Cannot Use TikTok:** Many government agencies are restricted from using TikTok due to national security concerns over data privacy and its connection to China-based company ByteDance.
- **Alternative Platforms:**
  - **YouTube Shorts** – Provides similar short-form video engagement while being backed by Google.
  - **Instagram Reels** – Offers TikTok-style videos within an already widely used platform.
  - **Facebook Reels** – Allows short videos within a trusted and regulated social space.
  - **Threads** – A text-focused alternative from Meta for discussions and community engagement.
- **Recommendation:** Agencies should evaluate platform policies and government guidelines before adopting any new platform.

Final Thoughts: Should Law Enforcement Adopt These Platforms?

- While these may be different platforms, your overall **goals and strategies** should remain the same. The principles of **transparency, engagement, timely communication, and public trust-building** apply across all social media channels.

- **Adapt content styles, but maintain consistency in messaging.** Whether it's a short-form video on YouTube Shorts or a community discussion on Discord, the core objective should always align with the agency's mission.
- **Prioritize Based on Community Usage:** Focus on platforms where your community is already active.
- **Test Before Fully Committing:** Experiment with low-risk, non-critical content before implementing full strategies.
- **Reassess Platform Effectiveness Regularly:** Social media trends evolve quickly—evaluate performance every six months and adjust accordingly.
- **Stay Flexible:** Adapt as necessary to technological changes and community preferences.

By exploring these emerging platforms, law enforcement agencies can expand their reach, strengthen community relationships, and ensure they stay ahead in the ever-changing digital landscape.

Appendix E:
Ideal Social Media Team

Introduction
A well-structured and well-staffed social media team is crucial for law enforcement agencies aiming to enhance their digital presence. While not all agencies have the resources to support a full team, this guide outlines an ideal structure for maximizing engagement, security, and crisis communication. Agencies can adapt these roles based on their specific needs, priorities, and available budget.

1. Social Media Director

- **Role:** Oversees the entire social media strategy, ensures alignment with agency goals, and coordinates all content and engagement efforts.
- **Responsibilities:**
  - Develop long-term digital communication plans.
  - Collaborate with law enforcement leadership to ensure transparency and public trust.
  - Manage crisis communication strategies.

2. Public Information Officer (PIO)

- **Role:** Acts as the official spokesperson, crafting press releases and handling media relations.
- **Responsibilities:**
  - Ensure all social media communications align with official agency statements.
  - Serve as the face of live-streamed events, press briefings, and major incident updates.
  - Manage relationships with journalists and community leaders.

3. Social Media Manager

- **Role:** Implements day-to-day social media strategies, manages content calendars, and ensures engagement with the public.
- **Responsibilities:**
  - Schedule and publish posts across multiple platforms.
  - Engage with the community, responding to comments and messages.
  - Analyze data metrics to improve performance and engagement.

4. Content Creators (Photo/Video Specialists)

- **Role:** Produces high-quality visual content to enhance engagement and storytelling.
- **Responsibilities:**
  - Capture and edit photos and videos for social media.
  - Create educational and awareness-driven short-form videos (e.g., YouTube Shorts, Instagram Reels).
  - Document law enforcement events, community engagement, and behind-the-scenes operations.

5. Graphic Designer

- **Role:** Designs professional and visually appealing content for announcements, safety tips, and campaigns.
- **Responsibilities:**
  - Develop infographics, crime prevention visuals, and branding materials.
  - Ensure consistency in visual storytelling and digital aesthetics.
  - Create engaging content tailored for different social media platforms.

6. Digital Engagement Coordinator

- **Role:** Monitors discussions, responds to public inquiries, and fosters positive community interactions.
- **Responsibilities:**
  - Actively engage in discussions to build trust and transparency.
  - Moderate comments and enforce community guidelines.
  - Facilitate interactive initiatives like Q&A sessions and live chats.

7. Cybersecurity & IT Specialist

- **Role:** Ensures the security of all social media accounts and prevents hacking, impersonation, and misinformation threats.
- **Responsibilities:**
  - Monitor for potential cyber threats, phishing attempts, and unauthorized access.
  - Enforce cybersecurity protocols, including multi-factor authentication (MFA).
  - Conduct regular security audits and ensure compliance with data protection policies.

8. Data Analyst & Performance Strategist

- **Role:** Tracks engagement metrics and performance to optimize content strategies.
- **Responsibilities:**
  - Analyze social media insights and trends to improve reach and impact.
  - Conduct sentiment analysis to gauge public perception.
  - Report key findings to leadership for informed decision-making.

9. Community Liaison Officer

- **Role:** Strengthens relationships between law enforcement and community groups through digital outreach.
- **Responsibilities:**
  - Act as a bridge between the agency and community organizations.
  - Plan online engagement initiatives, town halls, and community outreach campaigns.
  - Work with schools, businesses, and nonprofits to amplify public safety messaging.

10. Crisis Communications Specialist

- **Role:** Manages messaging during emergency situations, major incidents, or PR crises.
- **Responsibilities:**
  - Develop and implement rapid-response communication strategies.
  - Ensure accurate, real-time updates during critical events.
  - Prepare pre-approved messaging for various crisis scenarios.

Scenario 1: Small Agency (1-2 Staff Members)

- **Team Structure:**

  - Public Information Officer (PIO) or designated officer manages accounts.

  - Use scheduling tools (e.g., Hootsuite, Buffer) to plan content.

  - Automate emergency alerts via RSS feeds or pre-drafted templates.

- **Best Practices:**

  - Focus on high-impact platforms (Twitter for alerts, Facebook for community updates).

- Partner with city/county communications teams for additional support.

Scenario 2: Mid-Sized Agency (3-5 Staff Members)

- **Team Structure:**

  - PIO or Social Media Manager oversees the strategy.

  - Officers contribute content (behind-the-scenes, public engagement updates).

  - A dedicated crisis response lead for emergencies.

- **Best Practices:**

  - Rotate weekend/holiday coverage among team members.

  - Implement community engagement initiatives (Q&A sessions, town halls).

Scenario 3: Large Agency (Dedicated Social Media Unit)

- **Team Structure:**

  - Social Media Director

  - Content Creators (photo/video specialists)

  - Engagement Coordinator (responds to public inquiries)

  - Cybersecurity/IT Specialist (monitors for threats, account security)

- **Best Practices:**

  - Develop detailed crisis response playbooks.

- Train officers on content creation and online engagement.

- Use data analytics to refine strategy and measure success.

Conclusion

An ideal law enforcement social media team consists of a **diverse group of specialists**, each contributing unique skills to ensure **effective communication, public trust, and digital security**. While not every agency may have the budget for this full team, prioritizing key roles based on resources can significantly enhance online engagement and operational effectiveness.

Appendix F:
PPB Central Bike Squad

Introduction

Instagram: @PPBCentralBikeSquad

The **Portland Police Bureau (PPB) Central Bike Squad** has become one of the most effective law enforcement social media initiatives, striking a balance between professionalism, humor, and community engagement. Unlike standard police social media accounts that focus solely on announcements and crime prevention, this unit integrates **behind-the-scenes storytelling** with **engaging multimedia content**, helping to foster trust and transparency. The squad's dedicated social media officer provides a firsthand, authentic look at day-to-day policing, creating a **loyal following among the public, fellow officers, and even elected officials**.

This case study explores how **PPB Central Bike Squad** has used social media to build a **strong digital identity**, highlighting best practices that other agencies can learn from.

How PPB Central Bike Squad Built a Successful Social Media Presence

1. Consistency and Authenticity

One of the key factors in the squad's success is **consistent, authentic content** that aligns with its mission and audience. Their social media presence is not a one-off initiative; it is a **sustained effort**, with regular updates that keep followers engaged.

- **Dedicated Officer for Content Creation**: The unit has an officer who actively rides with the squad, capturing real-time footage, writing engaging captions, and interacting with the public.
- **Frequent Posts**: Regular updates include patrol footage, interactions with the community, and insights into policing strategies.
- **Authenticity Over Scripted Content**: Posts feel genuine and unscripted, helping to humanize officers and break down barriers between law enforcement and the community.

2. A Blend of Professionalism and Humor

The **PPB Central Bike Squad** strikes a **perfect balance between professionalism and lighthearted engagement**, making their content accessible and widely shared.

- **Humor as a Trust-Building Tool**: Posts often include **witty captions, funny observations from patrols, or lighthearted interactions** with the public, making the squad relatable.
- **Professionalism and Transparency**: While humor is present, it never compromises the **integrity or seriousness of law enforcement duties**. The squad regularly shares **educational posts about bike safety, crime prevention tips, and community initiatives**.

Example Post:

"Not all heroes wear capes. Some wear bike helmets and neon jackets. But in all seriousness—our squad is out ensuring pedestrian safety today. Give us a friendly wave (or better yet, obey the crosswalk signals). #BikeSquad #SafetyFirst"

Key Engagement Strategies

1. Behind-the-Scenes Content

People are naturally curious about what officers do daily. The **PPB Central Bike Squad capitalizes on this by providing an inside look into their work**, making law enforcement feel more transparent and accessible.

- **Videos of Bike Patrol in Action**: First-person perspectives make posts immersive and engaging.
- **"Day in the Life" Series**: Officers take followers through a typical shift, showing everything from bike maintenance to responding to incidents.
- **Equipment & Training Insights**: Content about the specialized gear and training that makes bike patrol unique.

2. Community-Centered Approach

The **PPB Central Bike Squad doesn't just post about their work; they engage with the community directly**. Their content highlights partnerships, neighborhood interactions, and community feedback.

- **Spotlighting Local Businesses & Events**: Officers regularly feature community hotspots and small businesses, further embedding themselves in the social fabric.
- **Recognizing Acts of Goodwill**: Whether it's a community member helping an officer or a positive interaction on patrol, these moments are shared to strengthen community ties.
- **Crowdsourced Engagement**: The unit encourages **followers to submit safety concerns, funny encounters, or positive feedback**, making the account interactive.

Example:

"Shoutout to the barista at [Local Coffee Shop] who made us an **espresso-fueled safety briefing** this morning! Community support keeps us rolling (literally). #SupportLocal #CaffeinatedCops"

The Impact of PPB Central Bike Squad's Social Media Presence

Increased Public Trust

- The squad's **consistent transparency and humor** have built a strong foundation of trust with the community.
- Engagement levels are high, with many followers expressing **positive sentiments toward the officers and their approach to public safety**.

Support from Leadership & Elected Officials

- The innovative engagement style has earned **recognition and support from police leadership and city officials**.
- Their posts often get **reshared by city council members and local leaders**, extending their reach.

Loyal and Growing Following

- Unlike generic law enforcement pages, the **Bike Squad has built a dedicated fanbase**.
- The **engagement rate per post is significantly higher** than traditional police department accounts.

Inspiration for Other Agencies

- o Other departments have **modeled their own digital engagement strategies** after the squad's success.
- o The approach demonstrates that **community policing and social media can work together** to change public perceptions.

Key Takeaways for Other Law Enforcement Agencies

The **PPB Central Bike Squad's success can serve as a model for other law enforcement units** looking to enhance their **social media presence**. Here are some **lessons learned**:

- • **Assign a Dedicated Officer for Content** – Having someone embedded in the unit ensures authentic, real-time updates.
- • **Use a Mix of Humor & Professionalism** – Humor helps build rapport, but should never overshadow core law enforcement messaging.
- • **Prioritize Transparency & Engagement** – Show behind-the-scenes content and engage directly with community members.
- • **Leverage Video & Multimedia** – Short-form videos, first-person footage, and interactive stories boost engagement.
- • **Encourage Community Participation** – Make social media a two-way conversation rather than just a broadcasting tool.

Final Thoughts

The **PPB Central Bike Squad** is an **outstanding example of how law enforcement can use social media effectively**—balancing **professionalism, relatability, and community engagement**. Their approach **humanizes officers, builds trust, and fosters strong community relationships**, making them a model for other agencies looking to modernize their social media strategies.

By adopting similar engagement tactics, **law enforcement agencies can transform their online presence from static updates to dynamic, community-driven storytelling** that resonates with the public.

Appendix G:
Officer Social Media Training

Purpose
This training framework provides law enforcement agencies with structured guidance for educating officers on responsible, ethical, and effective social media use. The program ensures officers understand best practices, risks, and departmental policies.

1. Training Objectives

By the end of this training, officers will:

- Understand departmental policies on social media use.
- Learn best practices for personal and professional social media conduct.
- Recognize legal and ethical considerations, including First Amendment rights.
- Develop skills for handling misinformation, criticism, and online engagement.
- Strengthen cybersecurity awareness to prevent unauthorized access and data breaches.
- Understand crisis communication protocols for official accounts.

2. Lesson Plan Structure

Each session includes:

- **Learning Objectives** – Key takeaways for the session.
- **Instructional Content** – Presentation of best practices, policies, and case studies.

- **Scenario-Based Exercises** – Interactive activities simulating real-world social media situations.
- **Discussion & Q&A** – Opportunities for officers to ask questions and discuss concerns.
- **Assessment & Certification** – A brief evaluation to ensure comprehension.

3. Key Learning Modules

Module 1: Social Media Policy Overview

- Agency's official social media policy
- Acceptable vs. unacceptable online behavior
- Differences between personal and professional use
- Case studies of social media violations and disciplinary outcomes

Module 2: Personal Social Media Conduct for Officers

- Privacy settings and personal security
- Avoiding controversial or politically charged discussions
- Engaging in responsible online interactions
- Understanding public perception and the impact of personal social media activity

Module 3: Handling Public Engagement & Criticism

- Responding to public criticism professionally
- Dealing with misinformation and online disputes
- When to engage, correct, or escalate comments
- Crisis communication and rumor control strategies

Module 4: Cybersecurity & Threat Awareness

- Recognizing phishing attempts and online threats
- Multi-factor authentication and secure password practices
- Reporting impersonation and hacking attempts
- Safe social media browsing habits for law enforcement personnel

Module 5: Crisis Communication for Law Enforcement

- Coordinating social media messaging during emergencies
- Using pre-approved response templates
- Working with public information officers (PIOs) for media relations
- Handling viral misinformation in crisis situations

---

4. Scenario-Based Training Exercises

Exercise 1: Social Media Review

Objective: Officers review public examples of law enforcement social media posts, identifying strong and weak practices.

Activity:

- Examine real-world posts from different departments.
- Discuss how tone, professionalism, and clarity impact public trust.
- Evaluate whether posts align with department policy.

Exercise 2: Handling Online Criticism

Objective: Train officers to respond effectively to public criticism on social media.

Activity:

- Role-play responding to different types of comments (misinformation, general criticism, hate speech).
- Discuss appropriate and inappropriate responses.
- Emphasize de-escalation and fact-based communication.

Exercise 3: Cybersecurity Threat Simulation

Objective: Recognize and respond to cybersecurity threats targeting law enforcement social media.

Activity:

- Officers receive simulated phishing emails and hacking attempts.
- Identify security risks and report them according to protocol.
- Discuss measures to prevent account compromise.

Exercise 4: Crisis Communication Simulation

Objective: Develop messaging strategies for real-time crisis situations.

Activity:

- Officers are given a simulated crisis (e.g., missing person, public emergency, major crime event).
- Draft appropriate social media updates using pre-approved templates.
- Role-play a press briefing or public Q&A session.

---

5. Assessment & Compliance Checklists

Assessment Quiz (Sample Questions)

1. What are the key differences between personal and professional social media use for officers?
2. How should an officer handle an online comment spreading misinformation?
3. What are the best cybersecurity practices to prevent unauthorized account access?
4. When should an officer report a social media security breach?
5. What steps should be taken before posting official department content?

Compliance Checklist

- Officers have reviewed and signed the agency's social media policy.
- Officers understand personal social media conduct expectations.
- Officers can identify and report online security threats.
- Officers have demonstrated proper handling of online public engagement.
- Officers understand crisis communication procedures and response templates.

6. Recommended Resources for Ongoing Training

- International Association of Chiefs of Police (IACP) Social Media Training
- FEMA Crisis Communications Certification
- Open-Source Intelligence (OSINT) Training for Law Enforcement
- Agency-provided cybersecurity awareness workshops
- Social media engagement best practices webinars

Conclusion

This training framework equips officers with the knowledge and tools necessary to navigate social media responsibly, professionally, and securely. Regular updates to the training program will ensure it remains aligned with evolving digital trends and public expectations.

Summary Guide

Introduction: Why Social Media Matters for Law Enforcement

Social media is no longer optional for law enforcement agencies—it's a critical tool for public communication, crisis management, and community engagement. This guide summarizes key best practices to help agencies effectively navigate the digital landscape, build trust, and stay ahead of emerging challenges.

1. Establishing a Strong Social Media Presence

- **Be Consistent:** Maintain a regular posting schedule with relevant, timely content.
- **Choose the Right Platforms:** Prioritize platforms where your community is most active (Facebook for community updates, Twitter/X for emergencies, TikTok for youth engagement, etc.).
- **Define Your Voice:** Be professional, transparent, and approachable—balancing engagement with credibility.
- **Train Your Team:** Ensure personnel understand best practices for digital communication, crisis response, and cybersecurity.

2. Engaging with the Public & Managing Criticism

- **Encourage Two-Way Communication:** Respond to public inquiries in a timely and professional manner.
- **Moderate Effectively:** Allow respectful discussions but remove comments that violate community guidelines (hate speech, threats, misinformation, etc.).
- **Correct Misinformation Promptly:** Use pinned posts, fact-checking graphics, and direct responses to counter false narratives.
- **Avoid Arguments & Defensive Responses:** Address criticism constructively and take complex discussions offline when needed.

3. Digital Trust & Crisis Communication Strategies

- **Be the First & Best Source of Information:** Share updates quickly and factually to prevent speculation and misinformation.
- **Develop Pre-Planned Crisis Messaging:** Have templates ready for emergencies, ensuring a coordinated response.
- **Use Video & Livestreams for Transparency:** Real-time updates during incidents build credibility and public confidence.
- **Collaborate with Trusted Partners:** Work with media outlets, community leaders, and influencers to amplify accurate messaging.

4. Future-Proofing Against Digital Challenges

- **Monitor Emerging Trends:** Stay ahead of AI-generated misinformation, deepfake threats, and encrypted social platforms.
- **Enhance Cybersecurity Protocols:** Use multi-factor authentication (MFA), conduct regular security audits, and train staff to detect phishing attempts.
- **Prepare for Platform Shifts:** Adapt to the growing importance of private groups, encrypted messaging apps, and alternative social networks.
- **Develop Long-Term Engagement Strategies:** Invest in digital literacy, AI awareness, and flexible social media policies to remain relevant.

5. Learning from Case Studies & Best Practices

- **Seattle PD:** Mastered crisis communication through real-time Twitter/X updates and misinformation management.
- **Rye Police Department:** Used TikTok to engage younger audiences with humor and relatable content.
- **Miami-Dade PD:** Set the standard for using social media during hurricanes, providing life-saving information.
- **Las Vegas Metropolitan PD:** Leveraged Facebook as a public safety hub with missing persons alerts and community discussions.

Final Takeaways: What Every Agency Should Remember

- **Be Transparent:** The public expects openness and accountability—regular updates build trust.
- **Stay Engaged:** Social media is about conversations, not just announcements—listen and respond.
- **Prepare for Digital Threats:** Cybersecurity is just as important as public relations—secure your accounts and verify information.
- **Use Video & Visual Storytelling:** People engage more with short, clear, and visually compelling content.
- **Evolve with Technology:** AI, misinformation, and encrypted platforms are changing the game—stay proactive.

By following these best practices, law enforcement agencies can effectively use social media to build stronger relationships with their communities, enhance public safety, and maintain credibility in the digital age.

About the Author

J.M. Ruby is a leading expert in **law enforcement social media strategy, digital communications, and public engagement**. With over **two decades of experience** in public sector multimedia, Ruby has helped shape the way government agencies use digital tools to build trust, share critical information, and engage with their communities.

Currently serving as a **Public Sector Digital Media & Web Manager**, Ruby specializes in **strategic communications, crisis response, and digital innovation**. His expertise spans **video production, social media management, and web development**, helping agencies navigate an evolving digital landscape where misinformation spreads rapidly, and public expectations for transparency are at an all-time high.

Ruby was among the **first in the nation** to integrate **social media into frontline law enforcement communications**, pioneering the use of **real-time engagement, self-deprecating humor, and behind-the-scenes storytelling** to humanize officers and increase public trust. His strategies have been **featured in national media**, and his agency's videos have reached **millions of viewers**, reinforcing the power of digital storytelling in public safety.

Before his work in law enforcement, Ruby served as **Director of Interactive Media** for an NBC television affiliate, where he gained a deep understanding of news media dynamics. His ability to **bridge the gap between traditional and digital media** earned him an **Edward R. Murrow Award** for journalistic excellence.

Beyond government communications, Ruby has also **built and managed large-scale social media accounts**, launched **successful digital brands**, and produced content that has been **featured by Apple and seen by millions worldwide**. His experience in **influencer marketing, digital branding, and content strategy** extends beyond public safety.

Through this **2nd Edition**, Ruby provides a **comprehensive, forward-thinking guide** for law enforcement and government agencies, offering the latest best practices in **social media engagement, crisis communication, and digital trust-building**. His goal remains the same: **helping agencies communicate effectively in an era where being the most reliable voice in the conversation is more important than ever.**

Index

www.ingramcontent.com/pod-product-compliance
Lightning Source LLC
LaVergne TN
LVHW081529050326
832903LV00025B/1691